The Lightworker's Source

The Lightworker's Source

An Enlightening Guide to Awaken the Power Within

Sahvanna Arienta

Author of *Lightworker*

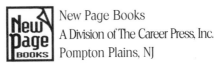

New Page Books
A Division of The Career Press, Inc.
Pompton Plains, NJ

THE LIGHTWORKER'S SOURCE
EDITED BY NICOLE DEFELICE
TYPESET BY GINA TALUCCI
Cover design by Lucia Rossman/ Digi Dog Design
Printed in Canada

To order this title, please call toll-free 1-800-CAREER-1 (NJ and Canada: 201-848-0310) to order using VISA or MasterCard, or for further information on books from Career Press.

The Career Press, Inc.
220 West Parkway, Unit 12
Pompton Plains, NJ 07444
www.careerpress.com
www.newpagebooks.com

Library of Congress Cataloging-in-Publication Data

Arienta, Sahvanna, 1966-

The lightworker's source : an enlightening guide to awaken the power within / by Sahvanna Arienta.

p. cm.

ISBN 978-1-60163-248-7 -- ISBN 978-1-60163-550-1 1. Parapsychology. I. Title.

BF1031.A75 2013

131--dc23

2012033789

This book is dedicated to Angelo Garcia.

Everywhere I go, every smile I see,
I know you are there smiling back at me.

Acknowledgments

This book could not have been written without the people who encourage, support, and inspire me each day. First, I would like to thank and acknowledge the entire publishing family at New Page Books. Thank you for allowing me this chance to have a voice and extend my message to the world. I am forever grateful for your professionalism, support, and encouragement throughout the entire process of writing *The Lightworker's Source.* A special thank you to my editor Nicole DeFelice, for your guidance and reassurance throughout the whole editing process.

I would also like to thank Denise Iwaniw for her contribution to this book and the hope and inspiration she brings to others all over the world through her work with The Gathering Thunder Foundation and in all she does. Gale St John, you are truly one of a kind. Your work with missing persons and their families is unlike any other. May God bless you and the sacred work you do all from the kindness of your heart.

My daughters, you knew when to give me inspiration and courage to fulfill my dreams and always make me proud. You have far surpassed my expectations and I am so honored to be your mother and your friend. I am also eternally grateful to the Universe for bringing me such a wonderful husband. Stephen, you are always on my side and there to encourage me to keep on going. You always believe in me, even when I don't believe in myself, and someday you will convince me that I really *am* a writer, I promise. My mother, who is my teacher, mentor, and best friend all rolled into one, thank you for being the one I can go to when I need clarity and focus. I don't know what I would do without you.

Last, but certainly not least, my guides and teachers who are not of this world. There are times when you shock and surprise me with information that comes from a sacred place. Thank you for guiding me in my work, and always helping me up when I am down.

Contents

Preface

People need a calling; they need to know why they exist. All Lightworkers have this inner urging to know. They feel a need to embrace a higher calling, but many just cannot find their focal point. For years, I have been helping people find out why they are here and how to manage the highly sensitive natures (that as Lightworkers) they have to live with. As a psychic (which has metamorphosed on its own into *spiritual counselor*), I have spent years helping my clients discover their roles, learn how to play their part, and understand that they are the star of their own lives. In my early career as a psychic, my focus was on telling people what was going to happen in the future. But as my clients' focus shifted, so did my career. They do not just want to know the future, they want healing, knowledge on their soul histories, and information on how to clear blocks to their ascension paths.

When I first began studying Lightworkers, I was shocked to see how many felt isolated, out of sync, and even somewhat worthless. Some acted out with addictions, self-doubt, and abuse, whereas others suffered silently, living life with a hollowness in their core that they just could not fill. They didn't understand the gifts they possessed, or the birthrights that come with the spiritual work they had done in their past lives. In fact, these same gifts were the cause of their great distress and anxiety. The cost of being super sensitive in such a harsh environment is high, and they had no conscious awareness of why they were in pain. It was as though they were sleepwalking through life, continually walking into walls and stumbling over furniture, and they suffered the bumps and bruises both physically and emotionally. But, just like turning on a light switch, if they could wake up and understand their sensitivities and learn to utilize them to help others, it would be transformational. Taking away the humanness was not easy, but Lightworkers needed to know themselves on a metaphysical level, moving past the perceived physical identity they had of themselves and examining their true essence.

When they were finally introduced to themselves underneath all the material matter, they began to understand why they suffered so much. They were grateful for a book that finally addressed their suffering and how to cope with it. When I wrote *Lightworker: Understand Your Sacred Role as Healer, Guide, and Being of Light*, so many people contacted me and were amazed by how many *ah ha!* moments could fit into one book! People related and they connected to the information in the book in such a powerful way that they declared reading the book a life-changing experience. The discovery of not only what their role was in their own lives, but within the collective finally made them feel as though they belonged. What a relief.

Because the book was released and Lightworkers had gained some vital knowledge of who they are, it was time to take the next step. *The Lightworker's Source* was written to help those who discovered themselves through *Lightworker* put into practice what they have discovered and learn how to implement their gifts. This is not a simple undertaking, but a conscious life change that must be incorporated in every action, thought process, and intent. Living as a Lightworker on the path to ascension (or oneness with God) is a journey that is not for the faint of heart, but this guidebook can be your roadmap.

This book will take you through the phases of awakening and guide you through them. These four stages can be difficult to navigate through, but the information I share can be very helpful. Once you have become fully conscious of your identity, it is important to begin mastering your role. A Lightworker who is not working toward healing and spreading light becomes depressed and filled with self-doubt. In this book I will also discuss how to utilize your gifts and different healthy Lightworker practices that will enhance your life. Lastly, we will discuss how to blend your human identity with your sacred role of Lightworker. Staying connected to the higher realms and living here on Earth can be a precarious balance. Through many hours of meditation, I have channeled these teaching from my guides and higher teachers, and it is their wish that you are assisted in achieving mastery of your role. I am just the humble massager, but also part of a collective army of healers, here to expand the light energy of the planet, and I am honored and grateful to be one among many.

Introduction
Being a Lightworker

Lightworkers are unique souls who incarnate here for special purposes. Some Lightworkers come here to be great spiritual leaders; some give us cures for diseases; others come just to share their light energy. Lightworkers from all universal dimensions have been descending to the earth in heavier waves for the last 100 years. Now with the new millennium and the coming of the Age of Aquarius upon us, Lightworkers' numbers have increased and we are now being inundated with a wave of highly evolved beings to balance the energy of the planet and help heal mankind. Consequently we see changes in humanity. People are becoming more enlightened and aware of the metaphysical. Holistic healing practices are now widespread and are slowly being accepted by the traditional medical field. People are searching and seeking out "unconventional" solutions to their problems, such as transcendental meditation, energy healing, or spiritual counseling. We are seeing changes in our children and young adults that indicates they are increasingly sensitive, which the older generation still has yet to learn to deal with, but that is coming as well. The signs are all around us that as a whole, our race is transforming. We are reaching a new level of awareness and the next phase in our evolution.

Within this new age of enlightenment, we are not without our guardians, teachers, and front-runners. Lightworkers are spirits who have spent countless lifetimes mastering the gifts of our Source Creator, and expanding their light energy. Lightworkers come from five learning planes of the universe (Earth is the first plane and the astral plane is the second, but neither are the place of origin for Lightworkers):

∞ Third plane: The realm of material detachment and spiritual adaptation.

∞ Fourth plane: The realm of beauty of sight and sound.

∞ Fifth plane: The realm of illumination and visionaries.

∞ Sixth plane: The realm of wisdom and connection to the higher-self.

∞ Seventh plane: The realm of oneness and unity.

As Lightworkers travel through these planes, they master the lessons of each one, and return to earth to share what they have learned. They heal our planet through the power of love, but their work here does come at a price for them. Many Lightworkers have a difficult time adjusting to life here. So acute and sensitive, they find the earth plane harsh and cruel. Lightworkers throughout history have shared their gifts with us and many suffered greatly, lost in the darkness of the earth plane and feeling the effects. Many Lightworkers choose to end their own lives or often times leave the earth in a tragic or violent way (Vincent Van Gogh or John Lennon, for example), but this need not be at all.

If you feel this inner urge to embrace your unique gifts and the practices that go with them, now is the time to wake up and share your glorious light with the world. Understand you are not expected to be born knowing you have work to do; Lightworkers aren't born with the conscious awareness of who they really are or why they have come, but they do feel a constant urge to be of service. As children, Lightworkers need to build the human foundation that will keep them grounded here on earth during their current lifetime. So it is necessary for Lightworker children to freely explore their humanness in order to adapt. Because Lightworkers must slowly acclimate to the earth plane, there is an awakening process they must go through. Like slowly being roused out of a deep sleep, it should be a gentle awakening. When their true identity struggles to emerge, they feel as if they have been dropped in a foreign country and no one speaks their language.

Every Lightworker who is struggling to emerge has a human side, which can easily work in harmony to help them fulfill the life they came here to live and help heal the planet. There is no need to feel out of sync or like you do not belong, and with the information contained in this book, you will more easily transition into executing your life purpose and mastery of your role.

Part I
Ending the Illusion

1
Awakening

As a Lightworker, you have lived through many lifetimes of spiritual work, which brings an expansion of your light energy. This advanced enlightenment and light energy creates a higher vibration of the spiritual body and an expanded healing energy that is desperately needed by humanity here on the earth. Before birth, all Lightworkers chose to share their healing energy during their incarnation. After much thought and discussion with higher teachers and guides on their plane of origin, the decision was made to make the ultimate sacrifice by incarnating to the earth and helping heal humanity from the effects of lower vibrational emotions such as fear, greed, or hatred.

The Choice Is Yours

All Lightworkers have the free will to decide whether to descend to earth and assist humanity or stay on the higher planes and continue their education and work there. So keep in mind, you have made this choice, but you are not alone. All over the world, Lightworkers are unveiling their authentic selves and emerging as the healers of the planet. As they awaken one by one, they will step into their roles as those who light the way for humanity. This choice is not always apparent or easily revealed.

Although Lightworkers are born unto this earth with their healing gifts and abilities inherent, these abilities may lay dormant for an undetermined time period. As they become aware of their true nature and begin to awaken, Lightworkers endure the challenging process of acclimation. Because Lightworkers incarnate with a form of amnesia or conscious *un*awareness of their authentic selves and their supernatural gifts, the awakening process can be traumatic. Many times, psychic abilities or spontaneous, other worldly interactions can transpire and frighten them to the point of suppressing of their extra sensory perceptions. My friend and colleague Denise Iwaniw, psychic medium and author, explains how she was able to deal with her Catholic background and the knowing she felt as a child in her book *Embracing the Mystic Within*:

Even as young as six I remember seeing faces when I closed my eyes at night. While most were pleasant, some were gruesome. I can still vividly remember one old man, one of the first who came to me, floating just inches above my single bed one evening as I wrestled with sleep. Like the leftover from an old B horror film, he stared directly at me, struggling as if to tell me something. But he wasn't some childish conjuring; a bad dream captured fleetingly and turned into mythic proportions. He was palpable, a bulky man with a broad face and red bulbous nose probably left over from many long nights in a bottle. Late fifties, I thought, thinning hair. His presence felt heavy, although the half dozen times he came to me he was always disembodied. He was struggling to get through, to make the leap. He never spoke.

I never told my parents.

After all, I was six and scared to death. What could they, or any adult offer me, but the sweet hush-hush there pats that only dismiss what is real and often what is really frightening?

My older playmates thought it strange that someone my age would be so preoccupied with ghosts. To this day, certain friends who knew me way back when never fail to remind me what a "weird" little child I was in their estimation. Those in spirit have always been a strong part of my life. I believe when you focus on something, all your energy flows into it, thus giving it power. Withholding energy means denying power.

As a human child with an open channel to the spirit world, when the two worlds spontaneously merge, it can be traumatizing and there aren't many (as Denise explains) who can offer much comfort.

To protect the divine essence of Lightworkers, they must incarnate to earth in a sleep state and only awaken when ready. They live with a conscious unawareness of who they really are. Their true selves are dormant or asleep until they are ready to begin the awakening process. This is a slow and precisely timed process that will gradually allow them to adjust to the density and harsh energies of the earth plane. Beings of increased light energy cannot just be placed on earth without a feeling of shock; they must be eased in gently, like being roused from a deep sleep state. It doesn't happen overnight because it is a process. The true Lightworker identity is being awakened slowly. The more easily one can let go of the illusion of the physical, the easier it will be to awaken.

Personally, I can relate to the feeling of living in this state of amnesia and what the result of living in that state means. I went through the first 30 years of my life filled with fear and anxiety. When I think back, it really was like being present in a dream, knowing it is a dream, and trying to wake up. I knew something was missing in my life and without the knowledge of my true self, I was immobilized with fear, anxiety, and the feeling that I was on a path to nowhere. I focused on all I did not have and was under the impression that material success was the only road to happiness. I always felt like an outsider and that I did not belong. Things got worse as I was so busy searching for physical satisfaction that I resisted my own spiritual awakening. Yet, somewhere deep down within my being (that persistent urge) I knew I had a higher calling, and until I experienced my awakening, I could not understand what it was.

Lightworkers must first go through a period of unhappiness or detachment, when they feel separate from the human family, feeling as though they do not belong or they are different. This identity crisis can be very isolating and send Lightworkers into a state of deep sadness. But what is really happening is their authentic selves are struggling with their human side, so it can finally emerge. When these feelings begin to stir deep within them, it is a sure sign that their awakening is not far off.

The Four Stages of Awakening

When Lightworkers live in this amnesia state, before they awaken to the divine intention of their lives, they are not conscious of their authentic selves. The trauma of awakening is similar to culture shock—the disorientation a person may feel when experiencing an unfamiliar way of life. To better explain; let's look at the four phases of awakening.

Phase 1: The honeymoon phase (incarnation and early life)

During this initial phase, the earth plane is seen as a new adventure. Childhood and the exploration of a new world seem fascinating. For example, when moving to a new country, a person might love the new food, the pace of life, and the locals' habits, and want to try everything. This phase is almost like sleepwalking, in that one operates on a different octave of consciousness than he would as a fully aware Lightworker. The *human* identity is in its most primal form and emerges as the front-runner while in this stage. This period is full of observations and new discoveries that will forever remain in the subconscious. This sleep state is necessary to incarnated Lightworkers, because this stage builds the human foundation that allows them to carry out their Lightworker mission. Lightworkers who are damaged or abused during this honeymoon period may have a more difficult time in awakening due to an excess of fear.

Phase 2: The negotiation phase (urging and resisting)

After some time, the differences between the divine light frequencies of Lightworkers' origins and the earth plane become obvious and create anxiety for them. The honeymoon phase eventually gives way to unpleasant feelings of frustration and stress as Lightworkers continue to experience the harsh energies of the earth plane. Their resistance becomes lowered, and this heightened sensitivity creates a disconnect from others and the planet as the spirit urges and the body resists. We often see this in the teen years or early 20s, when we see rebellion. Lightworkers in this stage often feel isolated and homesick as they begin to feel "different" and need to embrace a higher purpose. Extra sensory perceptions begin to emerge and can feel traumatic. This is a period of searching and testing the limits of their human side versus their spiritual nature.

Phase 3: The adjustment phase (awakening or awareness)

This is when Lightworkers finally surrender to their true identity. Awakening comes as a time of ultimate acceptance and surrender to the authentic self. At this point, fear is released and Lightworkers move easily toward the discovery of their unique and sacred purpose. There may be one or many catalysts into this phase. This does take some adjustments to the beliefs and habits they may have formed in earlier stages. Relationships and outdated behaviors geared toward physical or material satisfaction may fade away because they do not suit this phase.

There seems to be an internal clock set for awakening, which is predetermined before incarnating. This awakening is set for a certain point in Lightworkers' life paths, but can be altered or modified by circumstances associated with free will. For example, if you have a set awakening at the age of 35, but you choose to resist the awakening process, it can be delayed for a while, or even indefinitely.

There are many reasons Lightworkers may resist awakening and fear is always on the top of the list. Many Lightworkers resist their true calling because of beliefs that were instilled in them during their upbringing, such as religious beliefs or fears instilled by their parents. Also Lightworkers can become trapped in a certain phase and remain there, creating a vicious cycle of dysfunctional behaviors that makes it difficult to find your way out. Stages 2 and 3 of awakening bring out feelings that may be difficult to cope with and are the most perilous stages, but it is important to have an awareness of what is going on and to not quell these feelings with unhealthy habits or behaviors. Although awakening can be stressful, it ultimately does lead to the unveiling of your authentic self which brings about a more fulfilling way of life. As with any revelation, you must fully grasp and confront what is stirring within you to eventually get to the end or the mastery stage. Usually the difficult part comes when you reach the "negotiation" phase. The following unpleasant symptoms may occur:

∞ *Strange sensations in the head: Especially at the top of the head. This area (the crown chakra) is the opening that is the gateway to awareness of sacred information. The top of the head may tingle, as this area energetically begins to expand and prepare to receive divine information from the universe.*

∞ Feeling isolated or detached from the others: Many Lightworkers who begin to awaken live with a feeling of homesickness. They feel they do not belong and struggle for a place to feel at home. This is natural because Lightworkers have left the earth plane long ago for the glorious realms of love and light. Lightworkers have made a great sacrifice to return, but still they miss their plane of origin. As the unveiling of your authentic self occurs, you may feel isolated and different from others. At times, it is too painful to be around others. You may find yourself avoiding crowds or gatherings that seem joyful to others, and you wonder, what is wrong with me?

∞ Seeing or hearing things that others do not. Spontaneous connection with the spirit world will begin to occur more frequently and you may encounter some visitors from the other side as your line of connection to other dimensions begins to become clear. Psychic abilities are emerging and this can be scary.

∞ Unfulfilled feelings of wanting to heal the world. All Lightworkers have a vocation to heal the earth. As they awaken, they may feel a sudden need to help others, the environment, or even animals. Whatever spiritual calling you choose to answer will begin to beckon to you at this time. Conversely, this may create dissatisfaction in the work you have been doing and you may feel unfulfilled in your career path.

Feelings of restlessness and a need to make a career change can arise that the time of awakening. This is not to be rushed; as you awaken, you will naturally flow into your calling.

∞ Ending of relationships. During phase 2, you may have developed personal relationships that were not in alignment with your authentic self. These relationships could have been more egocentric in nature, (relating mainly to your mortality rather than your spirituality). As the awakening process occurs, these relationships will no longer suit you, and relationships based in a new energy without the same objectives will begin to form.

∞ Frightening dreams or images during meditation. As you open up to the collective consciousness, you may experience a strong connection to the pain and suffering of humanity. You may begin to experience prophetic dreams, visions, or even communication with the dearly departed during altered states of consciousness (meditation or even daydreaming). This is simply a sign that you are expanding your energy out into the collective and are sensitive enough to pick up frequencies that are not your own.

∞ Feeling detached from your physical body. At times, you'll feel ungrounded or as if you are about to leave your body. Lightworkers must often walk the precarious line of keeping their feet on the earth while their spirit is still connected to the higher realms. Literally functioning in two worlds is a skill that takes some getting used to. During the awakening process, the consciousness transforms into the new energy of a Lightworker, but the physical body sometimes lags behind, bringing on feeling disconnected.

∞ Periods of extreme fatigue. Your physical body will need more rest and need to "reboot" in order to harmonize with your elevated, spiritual self.

These effects can seem very unpleasant, but there are many positive results once you have reached the Awakening stage of your Lightworker path. Release old behavior patterns. Patterns that were based purely on the material world that do not enhance the spiritual body will begin to subside. Diet is one benefit. You will find as you awaken to your authentic self, poor eating habits will dissipate. You may decide to become a vegetarian, try a raw diet, or just become more cognizant of your nutritional intake. Beneficial dietary changes will help keep body, mind, and spirit in proper balance and you will naturally seek out this alignment.

Phase 4: The mastery phase (adaptation; living your sacred purpose)

In the mastery phase, Lightworkers are able to participate fully and comfortably on the earth plane. They have revealed their authentic selves and have learned to manage their sensitivities here on earth. They exhibit many of the traits they developed on the higher planes of consciousness, such as their healing powers and gifts of acute perceptions and the desire to share those generously with the world. The following may be experienced:

∞ *Shift in inner dialogue.* As you begin to open your channel to receive divine wisdom, you will be "downloading" more information from your teachers of the higher realms. As you move into this new and enlightened exchange of information, a new level of communication begins to take place. You will find your inner dialogue become more loving and tolerant of your own self and others around you. Insight and direction will come easily as your human consciousness is now accessible to the light beings of the higher realms who have been lovingly guiding you all along.

∞ *Symbolic or profound messages in dreams.* You will begin to gather knowledge and information that is useful to you in dreams or meditation. As you awaken and reach the mastery stage, you will become a clear channel for divine information and guidance that will enhance your life and those around you.

∞ *Finding other Lightworkers.* Relationships will form with other like-minded people and those who vibrate on the same energetic frequency as you. As you

> awaken and step into your role, you will naturally reach out for the energy of other Lightworkers and surround yourself with the support of those who are aligned with you. Feelings of isolation and detachment from others will fade away as you find your soul family of Lightworkers once again.

If you feel the inner urging to move forward and finally awaken to your true self, the best advice would be to surrender to it. Place your ultimate trust in the universe and allow it to happen. There is no need to rush. Remember that you are protected from the start and will only awaken when your time has come. Think of it as feeling energized from a restful night's sleep and being ready to get to work. There are no risks of pain or failure. There is only support and unconditional love from the universe. There comes a time in all Lightworkers' incarnations when they must recognize what is real (their spiritual self) and what is an illusion. There is nothing more liberating than discovering your authentic self and finally being free, knowing yourself as more than just the flesh in which the real you is encased.

2

The Dark Night of the Soul

The "dark night of the soul" is a term that dates back to at least the 16th century when Spanish poet and Roman Catholic mystic St. John of the Cross wrote of a poem of the same name, which documents the ascension process (or the soul's path to oneness with God). The dark night of the soul is not only a time of deep sadness, but of spiritual transformation, when you begin to shift your perception from what is perceived to what actually belongs to you and what is real. When you make this shift, the truth becomes clear: Only your spirit is real.

Usually the events that trigger the dark night experience are the loss of one or several things in the material or physical world, such as loss of a loved one, or being stripped of all material possessions. Suddenly you lose all things you once thought were important and the illusion of the material world falls apart. This loss brings you to a place where only what you cannot see or touch has real meaning. The dark night of the soul is really the death of this illusion (the idea that the physical world is forever) and your mourning period of this death. When you come to understand that all things can be taken from you, that everything gets old and dies, it is a sudden shock. You have to take safe haven, going inward to reach for your spiritual self to guide you out of the darkness. This inward focus is a necessity to all spiritual seekers and this is why it is a Lightworker rite of passage. Not to say that all Lightworkers must suffer to gain enlightenment, but all must come to the place where they recognize the illusion, or forever stay attached to the material world—that which is not eternal.

The Catalyst

There is always a catalyst or maybe more than one to send you into the dark night. It can be a divorce, the loss of a job, ill health, or any other loss that creates a void in your material or physical perspective. For me, it was the death of a loved one. At only 57, my father was diagnosed with terminal lung cancer and given only five weeks to live. I didn't want to lose my father; I wasn't ready to let him go. *How could a young man so full of vitality be taken away so quickly?* I wondered. *This is all there is? To work your whole life and have it all taken away from you, just like that.... What's it all for?* I continually questioned life and my priorities. What a shock to realize that all my father's work, all he had was no longer his, because he was gone! This experience (compounded by a series of other losses) sent me into a 10-year-long dark night of the soul. I missed the physical presence of my father and wanted that back. I mourned being able to see him, hearing his voice, and touching his face. Even though I believed in life after death, I still grieved and somewhere within me I stubbornly resisted the idea that his spirit was what was everlasting (not his body), and that we were now connected by a powerful source I could not see or touch.

If the loss is sudden or traumatic, it is more difficult to accept, and even being a psychic medium didn't help me in dealing with the loss of my father. Even though I was aware there was life after death, I still mourned the physical. Grieving a loved one's flesh and bone is to be expected, but we do always have assistance in overcoming this. A good example of how our loved ones try to assist us during our grieving process was something that happened just after my father passed.

My mother and I decided to take out the Ouija board and contact my father. We needed to connect with him and see how he was coping on the other side. He appeared rather quickly and began to communicate through the board. Finally I asked him, "Dad, where are you now?" I wanted to know if he was in heaven or in some kind of other dimension. Quickly the board spelled out "I am in the closet." The answer was strange, and I looked at my mother with a raised eyebrow. She thought a moment, and then she began to laugh. "Well this morning Dad's remains came from the funeral parlor. I haven't picked out an urn, so I put the box in my closet." So he was correct, his ashes were in the closet, but his true essence was somewhere else. This was typical of my Dad's sense of humor and strong validation that we were speaking with his spirit. He went on to say he was right there next to me, whole and as he always was, but his physical body was now cremated in a box in the closet. So this goes to show, the physical can be destroyed, but the spirit remains intact eternally.

The Death of an Illusion

When you experience your catalysts, these events can be so painful you may feel that there is nothing left for you. The sense of hopelessness can be overpowering and you may feel as if there is no way out of the pain you're facing. But remember, these painful events are just triggers to bring you to enlightenment. The dark night of the soul is a kind of death in itself, but nothing real has actually died there—only an illusion. Often it is part of the awakening process, which will usually come during phases two and three (as we discussed in chapter 1), and navigating through the dark night of the soul is like paving the pathway to the real you that exists under all the illusions of the physical world.

Reaching the dark night of the soul always comes at a time when the spirit has reached a certain level of edification and is ready to proceed to the next step in the ascension process. There are many reasons that a dark night of the soul experience presents itself, but within your ascension strategy, it is all planned and goes along with what you came into this lifetime to learn. In other words, the dark night only comes when you are ready for it. It can sometimes feel unexpected (or we may see it coming), but for all Lightworkers who are awakening, the day comes when we learn the physical manifestations we perceive around us are not eternal. Surviving the dark night is not about the events that catapult you there, but how you mourn the death of the illusion.

Brody's story

Brody was a high-powered attorney who seemed to have it all from the outside. His legal services were in high demand and he was quickly making a name for himself as a defense attorney. With his loving family and beautiful home, he seemed to have the world within his grasp and he had it all figured out.

One day, the practice he had worked so hard to build was being threatened by a minute error in his attorney trust account and a complaint to the bar association. As his worries mounted, he began to fall into a state of depression and hopelessness. The cases piled up on his desk and he found the work he once loved meaningless. Helping accused criminals get off the hook did not appeal to him anymore and he missed deadlines and court dates. Spiraling deeper, he eventually relinquished his law license without a fight. Others urged him to fight to keep his practice, but he felt overwhelmed by a feeling of emptiness and depression that he could not shake.

Although his world was crumbling, he felt a strange sense of relief when he closed his law practice and was hopeful he would embark upon another career that would bring him success once again, but he was soon hit with another blow. His wife asked for a divorce. Brody, with no more fight in him, left the beautiful home he worked so hard for and got a studio apartment in an urban area. Being out of work for so long, he took what he could afford. Brody spent five years in the small apartment and much of that time was spent wondering how he could fall so far and end up in the place he had. He felt such shame and embarrassment at the loss of all the great wealth he had acquired that he isolated himself from the people who really cared about him.

As he reminisced in his mind about the life he missed, he looked around the small apartment and began to view the possessions he had left as meaningless. "My television will eventually break," he thought. "My clothes will become outdated and worn. My cell phone will soon be antiquated." What would be left was just Brody, and he was not the same person anymore. The man who had it all had disappeared; he was just an illusionary identity. He found an old newspaper article documenting one of the highlights of his legal career when he won a precedent-setting case. The man in the article felt so foreign, as though he didn't even know him anymore and his life was just a story, just something to read about. He burned the article and cried for the loss of being that man.

Brody mourned the death of that man for a long time until one day he reached a turning point. Even though this man was not really "new," he was a stranger to Brody. This man he was getting to know was his authentic self, stripped of all possessions, the Brody who was real and no longer attached to material things. Soon his dark cloud lifted, and he began to embrace the urban community in which he now lived. He connected with people in his neighborhood on a level he never would have when he was a successful attorney.

As he began to feel comfortable in his life, he experienced a type of re-birth. Soon, he began to develop a deeper sense of purpose to a greater life than he had ever imagined when he "had it all." He saw that there were many people much deeper in hardship than he had ever been. Soon his embarrassment subsided, and he reached out to old connections to enlist their help in creating a day center for the city's homeless population. He became an advocate for the poverty stricken in the community and helped many people find food and shelter in the cold winter months. He was living a purpose-driven life that was not connected to anything that could be taken away or grow outdated. If he had remained a rich, successful attorney, he would have never faced the fact that his expensive suits and fancy cars were truly meaningless in the scope of things.

This is not to say you should burn all your material possessions and move to Calcutta and become the next Mother Teresa, but the dark night of the soul allows you to understand that the physical world has an expiration date (including your physical body) and your spirituality is eternal. This alters you're perspective of what is real and what is not.

Your Foundation

If you envision a huge mansion, with a brick exterior and a beautifully landscaped lawn, it all looks perfect. But if you examine it closely, and you come to see that the foundation it stands upon is crumbling, what you saw becomes a false perception of what the mansion really is—useless without a solid foundation. During the dark night, only what you can see or touch (or the bricks and lawn that looked so perfect from the curbside) is stripped away. The foundation or your authentic self (what Brody discovered when he released his attachment to the material things he had lost) remains. You may find getting down to your foundation can be very sad and dark, but what can result from renovating your foundation is known as *spiritual transformation*. During my spiritual transformation, I began to closely examine my own essence. I was introduced to my ego and my ego was comprised of nothing but pure fear. The fear of not being able to live up to others, fear of physical death, fear of sickness, fear of poverty, fear of being alone, they were all there, at my foundation, for me to face, and I began the process of sweeping my foundation clean (or confronting my fears). The only option I had to help me with this task was to surrender and put my fate in the Universe's hands.

At first I felt weak, as if I had given up, but then like a light bulb, I realized how much courage it takes to relinquish control and simply trust something that you cannot even see. I began to see that to incorporate this kind of ultimate trust into my life is akin to having the backing of something so powerful that nothing could defeat me, and then I felt unstoppable! What a relief to know that what people can see from the outside doesn't matter, and I did not need to live up to some kind of material or physical expectation of myself. When my fears no longer held meaning for me, the pieces of my life began to fall into place. I began to experience abundance, love, and vitality, because with my ego in check, with nothing to fear, I finally made room for joy in my life. This transforming experience is different for each Lightworker; it could take many days, months, or even years. Like me, you may have to come to a place of total surrender. It is a grieving process that only you can navigate through, but as you emerge from this period, you will achieve a higher state of enlightenment.

Find Yourself in the Darkness

As spiritual seekers, we are told to always look for the light, to align with the light energy of the universe and allow it to expand through our actions and our intentions. Many of us fail to understand that we must first know the darkness in order to live in the light. As painful as it is, the dark night of the soul is a catalyst for spiritual transformation, and without this powerful agent of change, we simply could not awaken to know our authentic self. It is only through working our way through the darkness that we find the light. As we navigate through the dark night, we are forced to seek out the part of ourselves that will guide us out. The part that is pure and directly connected to Source. Navigating through is not easy, and although you will emerge when you're ready, here are some ways to help you get through this transformational time.

Help yourself:

∞ Surrender. Now is the time for total trust in your higher self. Ultimate surrender to the process will get you through more quickly. You're not alone; there is always a light to guide you out. Allowing the process to flow smoothly without resistance will make it much easier for you. There is a bigger picture that you cannot see, and, remember, all things occur for the greatest good. Trust!

∞ Balance. As we experience the dark night, we may feel the need to go in one extreme direction or the other, either deep sadness or overdoing certain activities to allow us to live in a state of denial. We may attempt to counteract our pain by overeating, over-exercising, or numbing ourselves with medication or substance abuse. This creates an imbalance in the body, mind, and soul and halts your progress. Keep your physical body and mind balanced by eating right, getting proper sleep, and taking good care of yourself while embracing each day with the hope and faith that you will make it through this.

∞ Do Not Isolate Yourself. When we experience profound loss, we often feel alone and as though no one can relate. This is your journey, your ascension path to take, and no one can walk it for you. Still, this doesn't mean you must cut yourself off from the world. Surround yourself with people who sincerely care and can be supportive. Don't expect them to take the pain away, but reach out to them when you need some comfort.

∞ Don't feel victimized. Feeling victimized means you are looking at external causes for your suffering. Looking outside yourself takes away your power and causes you to focus on what's happening around you instead of looking inward. If you are in a period of spiritual transformation, see it as a gift. The dark night will pass, and you will emerge in an enlightened place.

∞ Stay focused. It is very important to stay aligned with the earth's energies during the dark night of the soul. It can be very easy to feel detached and disconnected from everything due to anxiety and perhaps depression. If you ever heard the expression "he's in another world," that is the perfect example of someone who is disconnecting to avoid transformation.

∞ Water is a very stabilizing element. Drinking water, taking baths frequently, and hydrotherapy keep you clear and focused. When bathing, add essential oils or flowers, which will enhance the effects of the water. Water creates a healthy flow of energy in your physical body.

∞ Grounding exercises can also be helpful. Lightworkers going through difficult times often want to escape the harsh energies of the earth, so it is necessary to ground yourself. As you sit in a chair, envision roots (like that of a tree) coming from your feet and firmly implanting themselves into the ground. Sit and hold this vision for as long you need to feel grounded to the earth.

∞ Ask For Help. All around you are beings of love and light wisdom waiting to help you. Angels, Spirit Guides, and deceased loved ones want to help you at this time. Request their gentle guidance now. This is not weak; it is extremely brave to trust in the higher powers that you cannot see.

∞ Although it is a painful process, the gift that comes along with the dark night of the soul is the understanding that your spirit is in fact one with Source. With the illusion of the physical world gone, your path is now clear for a huge shift in your life. Always remember that transformations are not easy, but each step forward brings more happiness and truth into your life. Navigating through the dark night is not for the weak, and only those who seek the most enlightenment experience it.

After this transformational experience, we now understand that we are all eternal, more than just flesh and blood. We now acknowledge ourselves as spirits having a human experience, yet we still must function within the confines of our physical body. Let's examine the limitations of our humanness and how to we may be able to overcome them.

3
Humanness Is an Illusion

As Lightworkers, we come to earth as highly evolved spirits who take human form in order to do real work for humanity. The spirit is the first and foremost aspect of our being because it is the only thing that is eternal. Yet the human form is the vessel that allows the spirit to carry out its plans. This tells us that there are actually two separate consciousnesses in one being that need to work together to carry out the mission.

To every Lightworker, there is a human side that needs to develop in order to carry the spirit (or higher-self) here in the physical world. But when the human awareness is permitted to dominate and forgets to nurture the spirit, Lightworkers become conflicted and begin to suffer identity crises. The spirit comes here with every intention of doing its work of healing and expanding the light energy of the planet, but the human side has its demands and sometimes can sidetrack the soul. The human awareness is oriented solely on the physical plane and only acknowledges what is material. It is born to the earth with primitive survival instincts and must be told (or trained) to allow the higher-self (which is much more evolved and enlightened) to be the dominate figure. If your human awareness functions without an awareness of its spirit, it becomes a materialistic, low-vibrational, dense matter with an unhealthy life force. But when the spirit is nurtured and comes to the forefront, the human side becomes vibrant, energetic, and ready to complete its mission, working harmoniously with the spirit. The only time this type of teamwork can take place is when the higher-self is allowed to take control of the incarnation. Then you are no longer limited to what you can see or the boundaries of a physical body, but the infinite universe, which is yours to explore.

As you awaken, you may find parts of your personality that are not in alignment with your higher purpose. This is to be expected because you were operating on a human level of awareness and became enslaved to human desires and yearnings. You are always going to have these human desires, but they should be secondary to your spiritual well-being. As a Lightworker, when you struggled to adapt, you felt a need to belong and wanted to fit in, and you more than likely allowed the human identity to dominate. This is where many Lightworkers lose their way and surrender to human weaknesses. They do not know their higher selves and struggle with an identity crisis for much of their lives as the human awareness weighs them down and makes it difficult to keep their frequency high. The battles are really internal as we struggle to rise above our human awareness and know the truths of what is beyond the material world. If we recall the theory of seeing the psyche structured into three parts: the Id, Ego, and Superego, all developing at different stages in our lives, the Id, the Ego, and Superego can pertain to Lightworkers as well. For Lightworkers, these three terms that were theorized by Sigmund Freud are significant to achieving mastery.

The Lightworker's Id

This is the persona that emerges in phase 1 of awakening. The Id must have its chance (during infancy and early childhood) to develop so the spirit can recognize the primal instincts of the human form. We need the Id in order to learn survival skills as a human. It sets the foundation of how to keep your human body functioning. The Id knows all the human gratifications and how to get them in an animalistic way. It knows no spiritual values because it strictly belongs to your human side. The Id doesn't concern itself with nurturing the spirit. During times of stress or crisis, it can resurface and try to take control. For example, if you are feeling out of sync with humanity, or are unable to execute your healing gifts, the Id may emerge to satisfy the primal human urges in an effort to counteract the pain of the inner spiritual being who is struggling to claim its identity. This is counter-productive because allowing the Id to take over and satisfy only physical gratifications can lead to addictions, sexual compulsions, or acts of aggression (usually taken out on themselves). These habits are totally out of alignment with your gentle, healing, Lightworker soul.

The Lightworker's Ego

Later in life (as the human awareness develops) if the spirit is not being nurtured and the Id struggles to emerge, the Ego will take over. The Ego strives to bring you only pleasure, and will (unlike the primal Id) devise plans and strategies that are more socially acceptable to attain pleasure. The issue with the Lightworker Ego is that it does its work through fear. Contrary to what may be believed, the Ego wants to be your friend. It strives to keep you safe, protected, and free from pain, but it does this through controlling your life using fear (the lowest vibration there is). The Ego is based in the physical world around you and doesn't see the bigger picture of your spiritual ascension path. The bigger the role Ego plays in your life, the less spiritually aware you become. The Ego seeks only pleasure and avoids any kind of pain at all costs. It will keep you from the pain of rejection by telling you things such as, "You're not good enough, so don't even try to get this new job." Ego means well, but its good intentions lower your vibration through the use of fear tactics, which blocks mastery of your Lightworker role.

The Lightworker's Super Ego

In this case, we will call it the spirit, soul, or higher-self (all meaning the same thing). The higher-self will supersede the other two identities when we achieve spiritual awareness. The higher-self knows you need the other two parts to survive, but will keep them under control and in their place. Whereas the Id and Ego are focused on material awareness and satisfaction, the higher-self knows the bigger picture and nurtures the spiritual side. The higher-self is far beyond the scope of fear; it is evolved far beyond pain and suffering. It understands pain doesn't exist when you are in sync with your creator and it understands the concept of oneness, so it doesn't know hate or jealousy. The higher-self only lives with unconditional love and compassion for all components of the Lightworker's personality. The higher-self is always there, but must remain quiet until you are ready for your awakening. This part of your identity is what needs to come forward and take the reins for you to achieve mastery.

In order to live a life that is not limited to our materialistic human awareness, we must allow the higher-self to take the lead in our lives. If we let the Id or Ego take over, we will remain at a very low frequency, which will never allow for expansion of our light energy, mastery of our role, or ascension. First, you must get to know who your higher-self is and become familiar with its intents and purposes.

Who is the higher-self?

The higher-self is your best friend, protector, teacher, and guide. The higher-self knows everything about you, from this lifetime, the previous lifetimes you have long ago forgotten, and lifetimes to come. Your higher-self holds all the answers your conscious mind searches for and is waiting to help you to your highest potential. Your higher-self is a direct extension of your Creator and is striving to ultimately achieve oneness. Your higher-self is free from the pain of loss and doesn't have the wounds your human awareness has incurred during the course of living. It is pure and unadulterated love and compassion; it knows the deepest truths of who you are. The authentic self is always there, waiting for the chance to come forward and help make your life beautiful. Your higher-self is all knowing, eternal, and comprised of only love.

Now is the time to invite your higher-self into your conscious awareness and allow the higher-self the role in this life that it should have. Connecting the higher-self and your human awareness is something that takes some practice, but must be achieved in order for you to get to the mastery stage of your Lightwork.

Getting to know your higher-self

Your higher-self is never far off, just beyond the door of your human awareness, waiting to offer support and assistance. Here are some ways that your human awareness can connect with your higher-self and allow it to become the dominant force in your life.

Listen to your intuition

You intuition is your higher-self guiding you. If you ever heard that little voice inside your head telling you not to do something, that is your higher-self. Many of us do not trust the voice of the higher-self and disregard its messages. But if you had a friend who knew you better than you know yourself, would you listen to them? Think of your intuitive feelings or hunches as advice from a friend who only wants the best for you.

Meditation

Meditation opens the channel to communication with the higher-self. Meditation can occur anytime or anywhere. You do not need to sit in a lotus position and chant to receive messages from your higher-self. If you're feeling confused and need guidance, quiet your mind for a moment and listen to the messages that come. During meditation, your higher-self may communicate to you in different ways. Do any physical feelings come to you? Do you feel sick, uncomfortable, happy, or joyful? Are you hearing anything? Do any images or memories flash through your mind? These can all be messages that have real meaning. It is up to you to pay attention and pick up on them. These subtle messages can be your higher-self sending you signals to tell you if you're on the right track or not. Take each and every sensation, message, or image you get and use it for guidance. Write them down. If you don't understand them in the moment, their meanings may become very clear later on.

Trust in your higher-self

When we have a trusted friend, we turn to that person in times of need. This is what you must do with your higher-self. When you are in need, trust that the answers given will be in your best interest. Remember, the Id and the Ego may want something else and may stamp their feet and not want to hear it. Although the answers may not be what your human consciousness wants, know that the higher-self knows what is best and will fight the Id and Ego to keep you on the right path. The higher-self knows the big picture and knows so much more than the primal Id or fear-based Ego. I have this happen many times with my clients. They already know the answers, but they refuse to accept what is true. They do not trust their higher-selves.

When you feel lost or don't know what to do, invite your higher-self in to take over. You will immediately feel a burden lifted off your shoulders when you do. Have ultimate faith and trust that all is right with the world and nothing can harm you. Because judgment is a human emotion, the higher-self would never consider you weak or a quitter. If you invite the higher-self in to resolve a problematic situation, you will see yourself dealing with it with loving compassion and forgiveness, which only brings healing and resolution for all involved.

There is more to you than just what the human part knows. To allow your higher-self to take the reins and be the dominate force in your life will shift your perspective from what is just instinctual in nature (the physical self) to what is more consciously aware of your true nature (the spiritual identity). The two work hand-in-hand, but the conscious awareness must take the forefront.

The first step is to shift the perception of yourself that exists within the limits of your humanness. Yes, you are human and in physical form, but your true essence is energetic, which is without limitations. You are a spirit having a human experience, not a human having a spiritual experience.

There is a certain tone and verbiage to the voice of the higher-self and you must learn to recognize it. The voice of the higher-self is loving and supportive. It is never self-deprecating and it doesn't instill fear or threats. So any negative internal dialogue that you experience is not coming from the higher-self. You can easily be tricked by the Id or Ego and follow their advice. Know the voice of the imposters and shut them down before they even get a chance to invade your energy.

Your Body the Courier

As we travel our ascension path or raise our vibration, how does our physical body react? If the physical body is only dense matter, does it elevate as well? We need our physical body to function within a solid material plane and it cannot be left behind when the life force (or spirit) rises up. When we start moving into a higher vibration in our lives, our bodies will follow suit. This is why, when awakening occurs, foods, drinks, and preservatives we ingested our whole lives will make us sick, and we'll feel a need to change our eating habits. It is very important to appreciate and take care of the body, because it is the vessel through which you will do your life's work. The physical body *is* more than just dense matter; it has its own primal level of consciousness as well. The physical body must be aware of how to function and stay alive, but its awareness is governed by the spirit or life force contained within it. It reacts to what the spirit tells it. If the spirit is weak or neglected, the body will act in a primal way and take all it desires for pleasure purposes. It will become out of shape, sluggish, and unhealthy. But if the life force (or spirit) is strong and well-balanced, the body will be healthy, active, and free of disease. It will take its cues from the spiritual essence by which it is being used as a vessel. So the spirit is really the boss in this partnership. The body is merely there do the spirit's bidding and to carry out all its intents and purposes.

If we can grasp this concept, we can begin to understand how we can bypass the constraints of our humanness with the understanding that the spirit is without boundaries, therefore it is not confined by the body's limited awareness. The spirit has the power to rule over the body, creating optimal health, delaying the aging process (the body does have an expiration date, but it can be extended), or even curing ourselves of diseases. We can have optimal health and vitality while here on earth. There is no need for sickness or disease. We just need to find that connection between spirit and body and make sure the spirit is sending the body the right commands.

Healthy spirit, healthy body

There are many ways to nurture the body that we are all aware of, such as eating properly, exercising regularly, and resting adequately. Still, we can do all this and still develop diseases and debilitating conditions of the body.

If a person has unhealthy habits or addictions, they stem from an unhealthy spirit. Addictions and unhealthy habits are usually spiritually based and come from spiritual wounds or injuries that have gone unhealed. If the spiritual body is healthy, the body will automatically follow suit and be healthy as well.

You can nurture your spirit in many ways. The first and foremost way is to emanate unconditional love. Having loving compassion for yourself and others makes you unstoppable. What can hurt you if you approach each person or situation with love and compassion? In the spirit world, there are no right or wrong judgments. Everything contained within the universe is one and the same. Here's another way of looking at it: If the universe is complete and all things contained within it are one, then all things must be loved and accepted equally. Judgment is a human emotion that doesn't exist in the grand scheme of universal energy. Only love and compassion does.

Another way to nurture your spirit is to have a strong faith system. When you have no faith, you live with the belief that only what your eyes can see is all there is, living with the certainty that there is no greater plan or you have no purpose. This mindset causes us to attach to what is not real—the material. Attaching to the material brings on fears of loss because it can all be taken away and nothing eats up the spirit like living a fear-based life.

Another way to keep the spirit healthy is to set your intentions high. Ask yourself why you're doing what you're doing at any given time. If you're not doing something out of love, then chances are, your intentions are not high and this lowers your spiritual vibration. You must also learn to interact with others who are not as high-vibrational and still keep your frequency up. This may not be easy because we all have effects on the energy of those around us. Being around negative people or environments will wear you down. So it is best to stay clear of them. Remember everyone and everything in the world holds universal energy, and universal energy is a double-edged sword. It can be light and uplifting, or it can be dark and dismal. Lightworkers must make a conscious choice every day to align with the light side of source energy or they will deplete their light energy while here on earth. Nurturing your spirit is a daily practice that takes some work, but once you get into the habit, it will come naturally and everything else will just feel wrong.

Humanness and Unnecessary Boundaries

Your human perception is focused solely on the material world and your fear of losing it. Attaching yourself to physical pleasures or material satisfactions can lead to addictions, compulsions, and fear-based behaviors that keep you earthbound. Once the body grows tired and lets go of your life force, you will find it hard to move on. Earthbound spirits are people who have died and refuse to move on because they are attached to their human, fear-based perceptions. As we will discuss, there are many beautiful realms for you to inhabit and the earth plane is not one of them. Once you have completed your work here, you should be free to move without any material attachments, but if you remain focused on your humanness, or all that is material, you will not want to leave the earth plane, making ascension impossible. It is necessary to have the ability to trust what you cannot see. This will take your focus out of the physical plane and into the metaphysical planes where there are no limits or boundaries.

Part II

Creating a Healthy Energy Flow

4

Your Energy Portals

The word *chakra* in ancient Sanskrit translates into "wheel." Chakras have been described as spinning wheels that revolve and constantly move energy throughout our physical and nonphysical structures. Strategically placed throughout our bodies, there are seven chakras that align with different areas of our life. Much of the content of this book pertains to maintaining your energy, and keeping it healthy and balanced, so it is important to know how source energy actually revolves, cycles, and recycles through your body.

What Do Chakras Do?

The chakras' main function is to accept and cycle life force (or source) energy throughout your spiritual and physical body. By doing this, they assist us in holistic transformation by constantly moving and rejuvenating our life force for us. Source energy doesn't just randomly channel through you, it is organized and systematized by these spinning wheels throughout your body. The chakras, being the conduit of your life force, must flow clearly and freely and if they are not balanced, free of debris, or cleared, your basic life force will be slowed down. As you read the following descriptions, you will learn the physical, emotional, and spiritual diseases that can come with each specific chakra when blocked, wounded, or beaten down. Also there is a powerful correlation between your chakras and endocrine systems, which, if not properly balanced and maintained, can lead to physical illnesses. Energy must flow through the chakras freely as they create harmony with not only body, mind, and spirit, but the energy of the universe as well.

The Seven Chakras

Here, we will talk about what functions they are associated with, their physical locations, the purposes they serve, and the type of knowledge that is stored in each of the chakras.

The first chakra: root chakra

∞ Color: red

∞ Physical location: base of the spine

∞ Area of body governed: spinal column, legs, feet, rectum, immune system

∞ Glands associated: *reproductive glands, ovaries/testes*

∞ Purposes: *grounding, connecting, and linking with others and the earth plane*

∞ Diseases associated: *sciatica, hemorrhoids, constipation, varicose veins, rectal tumors, depression, immune-related disorders. All conditions labeled attention deficit disorders.*

∞ Holds within: *familial beliefs, loyalty, instincts, physical pleasure or pain, touch. Primal urges, self-esteem, community, feelings of belonging and family, fears of poverty.*

This chakra is located at the base of the spine. It is the grounding force that allows us to connect to the earth energies. Trauma or deprivation of love from the age range of birth to 6 years of age can greatly effect energies held within the root chakra and create deep emotional voids. Your root keeps you in alignment with your physical body when you find yourself energetically disconnecting or floating in outer space. Think of it as compared to the roots of a tree, firmly entrenched into the ground. Many Lightworkers find it difficult to adjust to the earth plane and precariously try to balance alignment with different dimensions. Because they are so divinely connected, Lightworkers will have a tendency to "space out" or feel detached and may struggle to stay focused in the physical, but paying special attention to your root chakra will keep you grounded and help you to concentrate here on earth.

The second chakra: the sacral chakra

∞ Color: orange

∞ Physical location: lower abdomen to the navel

∞ Area of body governed: sexual organs, stomach, upper intestines, liver, gallbladder, kidney, pancreas, adrenal glands, spleen, middle spine

∞ Glands associated: adrenals

∞ Purposes: emotional connection, creativity, manifestation, co-creating, relationships, releasing outdated behaviors

∞ Diseases associated: gynecological problems, reproductive challenges, pelvic pain, libido, and urinary problems and infections

∞ Holds within: duality, magnetism, controlling patterns, emotions (joy, anger, fear, and guilt, and obsessions with sex, power, and control).

Located just above the navel, this chakra allows us to release and find a balance in our lives. Trauma from ages 6 to 12 can be stored here. Toxic energy here can directly affect our sense of self-worth, governing relationships and sexuality, partnerships, and the ability to make changes in our life though making good choices.

The third chakra: the solar plexus

∞ Color: yellow

∞ Physical location: solar plexus/pit of the stomach

∞ Areas of body governed: stomach, upper abdomen, rib cage, liver, gallbladder, middle spine, spleen, kidney, adrenals, small intestines

∞ Glands associated: pancreas

∞ Purposes: to express emotions, sense of self, and willpower

∞ Diseases associated: stomach ulcers, intestinal tumors, diabetes, pancreatitis, indigestion, hepatitis, cirrhosis, adrenal imbalances, arthritis, self-esteem issues, fear of rejection, self-doubt, self-image issues, indecisiveness

∞ Holds within: personal power, individuality, consciousness of self within the universe (sense of belonging), intuitive powers

This is the area that defines our sense of personal identity. Toxic energy from ages 12 to 18 can be stored here and the perception of "self" developed during puberty can remain here. The solar plexus stores willpower, confidence, and sense of empowerment. Intuition is here and this is where we get our "gut instincts" that should guide us through our everyday lives.

The fourth chakra: the heart chakra

∞ Color: green, pink

∞ Physical location: center of chest

∞ Areas of body governed: heart, circulatory system, blood, lungs, diaphragm, thymus, breasts, esophagus, shoulders, arms, hands

∞ Gland associated: thymus gland

∞ Diseases associated: immunity disorders, heart conditions, asthma, lung and breast cancer, thoracic spine, pneumonia, upper back, shoulder problems. Lack of self-confidence and self-love, despair, hate, envy, fear, jealousy, anger

∞ Holds within: the healing power of unconditional love for yourself and others.

This is really where Lightworkers need to live centered from. This chakra is the focal point of healing through unconditional love, which is the main purpose for the Lightworker's incarnation to earth. The heart chakra allows giving and receiving love, compassion, and our connection to all forms of life. Toxic energy can be stored here from traumatic events between the ages of 18 and 25. Situations such as divorce, separation, grief through death, emotional abuse, abandonment, and adultery, create wounds that, if not healed, affect all our future love-related interactions.

The fifth chakra: the throat chakra

∞ Color: blue

∞ Physical location: throat, neck region

∞ Area of body governed: throat, thyroid, trachea, neck vertebrae, mouth, teeth, gums, esophagus

∞ Gland associated: thyroid

∞ Diseases associated: sore throat, mouth ulcers, scoliosis, swollen glands, thyroid dysfunctions, laryngitis, voice problems, gum or tooth problems, TMJ, blocks to personal expression and creativity, addiction, criticism, fear of decision-making (choices), lack of authority

∞ Holds within: clear speech and fluency of communication, truth

Located in the hollow center area of the throat, the fifth chakra works proficiently in relation to how openly we express ourselves. It is our clear connection with all forms of communication. It tends to develop and come to its full power within the age range of 25 to 40. We have all experienced that "lump in our throats" when we cannot find the words to express ourselves or perhaps even suppress our own emotions by not speaking our truth, and that is when our throat chakra is energetically blocked.

The sixth chakra: the third eye chakra

∞ Color: indigo

∞ Physical location: center of the forehead

∞ Area of body governed: brain, neurological system, eyes, ears, nose, pituitary, pineal glands

∞ Gland associated: pituitary

∞ Diseases associated: brain tumors, strokes, blindness, deafness, seizures, vertigo, learning disabilities, spinal dysfunctions, panic, depression, fear of truth, discipline, evaluation, concept of reality, confusion

∞ Holds within: clairvoyance, wisdom, mental facilities, intellect

Located just above the brow in the center of your forehead, this is the portal for your extra sensory perceptions, where you can receive guidance and tune into your higher-self. These abilities come through to full fruition between the ages of 25 and 40. Telepathy, clear channeling of information, and the ability to see beyond the physical are all located within the portal of the third eye.

The seventh chakra: the crown chakra

∞ Color: violet, white

∞ Physical location: top of head

∞ Area of body governed: top center of the head, midline above the ears

∞ Gland associated: pineal

∞ Diseases associated: diseases of the muscular system, skeletal system, and the skin; chronic fatigue syndrome; hypersensitivity to light, sound, and environment; lack of purpose; loss of meaning or identity; selflessness; inability to see the bigger picture in the life stream; uninspired

∞ Holds within: divine wisdom, our oneness with the universe, all that is

The seventh chakra sits at the top of the head, directly in the area of the fontanel where it is said the soul enters at birth and exits at death. Closing shortly after birth, it gradually begins to reopen at its broadest between the ages of 55 and 70. It is the opening to receiving divine communication and information from your Source Creator, which brings spiritual transformation, awakening, and ultimately oneness. It is through this area that source energy is dispersed from the universe and into the lower six chakras.

Keeping Your Chakras Cleansed and Balanced

When our chakras are out of balance, it can have a profound impact on our physical, emotional, mental, and spiritual health. When they are out of balance or alignment, harboring excess toxic energy from trauma or stagnating the life force that fuels our bodies, our lives are likely out of balance as well. Many diseases and conditions can result from an unhealthy chakra system. Also, if one is not working properly, all chakras will be affected. They all need to work in sync. If you do not maintain your chakra system, you will find yourself sluggish, lethargic, accident-prone, and maybe even sick. You will also lack the vitality for life you will need to expand your light energy.

There are many ways you can keep your chakras functioning properly. In order for them to do their jobs properly, they need some maintenance.

Colors

Each chakra has a specific color aligned with it. These colors activate the corresponding chakra to keep it healthy and happy. If you feel you need to work on your heart chakra, wear pink or green. If you want to work on your expression (throat chakra) wear blue, and so on. You can wear jewelry or accessories of that color, or even paint a room that color. It's simply a matter of bringing those colors into your everyday life.

Crystals

Crystals are stones that have a powerful healing vibration. This vibration can help the chakras become activated (moving again) and aligned. To use the crystals, lie down on your back and place the crystal or crystals on the chakras that need to be activated. Staying in this position for about 15 minutes, the crystals will quickly re-align the chakras. Here are some suggestions for crystals that work well with specific chakras.

- ∞ First chakra: Hematite
- ∞ Second chakra: Carnelian
- ∞ Third chakra: Citrine
- ∞ Fourth chakra: Rose quartz
- ∞ Fifth chakra: Sodalite
- ∞ Sixth chakra: Tiger eye
- ∞ Seventh chakra: Amethyst

Water

Water is the grounding force of the universe. Making sure you are well hydrated and getting enough water is important to maintaining a healthy charka system. Also baths and showers will clear away toxic energy you have accumulated after a tough day at work or with the kids. Think of it as diluting your energy and flushing it clean.

Exercise

It is important to keep the body fluid and active as well. The energetic body and physical body need to stay in harmony in order to achieve balance. So a regular exercise routine is needed. Even walking for 30 minutes a day will get things moving. Sedentary living will slow your chakra system down quickly.

Meditation

There are many chakra cleansing and balancing meditations you can practice once or twice weekly to keep yourself in alignment. These are simple and really don't need to take up much time. Set aside 15 minutes twice a week for chakra meditation.

Chakra-balancing meditation

Sit comfortably on a chair with your hands on your legs. Make sure your spine and shoulders are aligned. Your posture is important, because any slouching or slumping can obstruct the energy flow coming in and out of your chakras. Practice the purposeful breathing technique. We are going to utilize color and breath in this meditation. Visualize your breath as the color of the chakra you are working on.

1. *Focus on your foot chakra. Visualize the chakra as a bright red ball spinning clockwise. Breathe in red, breathe out red. Keep this focus for approximately two to three minutes until you feel a clearing. Visualize the spinning red ball being cleansed by a crystal clear flow of water washing over it. Continue to visualize until you feel a cleansing has taken place.*

2. Focus up the abdomen to the sacral chakra. Visualize the chakra as a bright orange ball spinning clockwise. Breathe in orange, breathe out orange. Keep this focus for approximately two to three minutes until you feel a clearing. Visualize the spinning orange ball being cleansed by a crystal clear flow of water washing over it. Continue to visualize until you feel a cleansing has taken place.

3. Focus on the solar plexus chakra. Visualize the chakra as a bright yellow ball spinning clockwise. Breathe in yellow, breathe out yellow. Keep this focus for approximately two to three minutes until you feel a clearing. Visualize the spinning yellow ball being cleansed by a crystal clear flow of water washing over it. Continue to visualize until you feel a cleansing has taken place.

4. Focus on the center of your chest, or the heart chakra. Visualize the chakra as a bright green ball spinning clockwise. Breathe in green, breathe out green. Keep this focus for approximately two to three minutes until you feel a clearing. Visualize the spinning green ball being cleansed by a crystal clear flow of water washing over it. Continue to visualize until you feel a cleansing has taken place.

5. Focus on the hollow of your throat, or the throat chakra. Visualize the chakra as a bright blue ball spinning clockwise. Breathe in blue, breathe out blue. Keep this focus for approximately two to three minutes

until you feel a clearing has taken place. Visualize the spinning blue ball being cleansed by a crystal clear flow of water washing over it. Continue to visualize until you feel a cleansing has taken place.

6.	Focus on the center of your forehead, or the third eye chakra. Visualize the chakra as a bright indigo ball spinning clockwise. Breathe in indigo, breathe out indigo. Keep this focus for approximately two to three minutes until you feel a clearing. Visualize the spinning indigo ball being cleansed by a crystal clear flow of water washing over it. Continue to visualize until you feel a cleansing has taken place.

7.	Focus on the top of the head, or the crown chakra. Visualize the chakra as a bright violet ball spinning clockwise. Breathe in violet, breathe out violet. Keep this focus for approximately two to three minutes until you feel a clearing has taken place. Visualize the spinning violet ball being cleansed by a crystal clear flow of water washing over it. Continue to visualize until you feel a cleansing has taken place.

8.	Finally, see white light flowing down from the universe through your crown chakra, all the way through all the other chakras, and finally into the earth. Visualize yourself with a glowing white light surrounding you and the chakras within your body spinning brightly (in their chosen colors). Hold this for two to three minutes.

Doing this meditation one or two times a week will keep your chakras cleansed and actively recycling your energetic body. Remember that your chakras organize, systematize, and energize your life force, and it is important to stay mindful of their health and maintenance just like you would anything else that is of importance in your life.

5
The One-Way Flow

As we discussed, Lightworkers harbor an excess of light energy, but there are many hues within the universal energy field that make it complete. Lightworkers happen to align more on the light side than other people. Everything within the universe has polarities, including universal energy, and there is a huge space of gray in between the light and the dark. Just as the energy of the universe needs balance to maintain stability for everything contained in it, Lightworkers must stay somewhere in the middle (or grey area) to maintain balance. Many Lightworkers fall into the trap of either functioning on one side of the energetic pole, or polarizing their energy and creating a one-way flow of light energy going out. For example, the Lightworkers who feels they must serve and heal at all times create a one-way flow of energy only going out, and they will become depleted. This quickly creates polarization to the dark side, leaving these Lightworkers vulnerable to depression, addiction, or dysfunctional relationships.

Polarizing into the light side can quickly send you in the opposite direction, which can sometimes be a difficult place to emerge from. At times, Lightworkers tend to feel they need to give and give and never take anything back in return. Many Lightworkers feel guilty taking in energy, or fearful they are becoming self-serving or selfish, but these feelings are unwarranted. There needs to be a steady balance of energy coming in and going out to keep your energetic flow in perfect sync. The stability this flow brings puts you in the best position to practice self-mastery.

Polarization

If we look at all universal energy, it must ebb and flow in order to be balanced. If we have what is called a one-way flow, we create a "food chain" in which the energy that flows through a one-way stream is transferred by organisms who are "eating" and then "being eaten." When Lightworkers create a one-way flow of energy in their lives, they dwell at the bottom of the food chain and are devoured, energetically speaking. Lightworkers who travel a road of only servitude, who think of others first, no matter what harm this might bring into their own lives, are only putting out light energy, but never drawing it in. They may rationalize what they are doing as helping others, but in actuality, they are throwing the entire energetic scale off-kilter. Naturally, they will come to an end point and have nothing left to give.

Depletion of light energy creates many undesirable side effects for the Lightworker and deters them from their purpose. For example, I worked with my student Cecilia for many years, developing her intuition and honing her Lightworker gifts before she opened a healing practice. She was a child abuse survivor and spent much of her adult years in dysfunctional relationships prior to her awakening. During the awakening process, she began to understand the part she took in her own misery. For her entire life, she worked at trying to fix things for others or endure their suffering for them. When she was a child, she witnessed her mother's abuse by her stepfather and she would take the role of an adult by nursing her mother's wounds or trying to take the blame. She always felt a tremendous amount of guilt when someone around her was struggling if she could not relieve their suffering, and feared being abandoned by them if she couldn't make it right, as she was abandoned by her biological father. As an adult she discovered she actually enabled her alcoholic husband by making excuses for him and never holding him responsible for his actions. She became physically ill with chronic pain and suffered depression.

When she came to me for guidance, we discovered her Lightworker identity and recognized the constant urging she felt all her life to heal everyone around her. Without a real handle on her authentic self, she fell into the Lightworker trap of only giving out light energy and creating a one-way flow, which eventually caused her to polarize into the darkness, subsequently bringing on her illnesses. As we uncovered her true nature, I worked with her in actually learning to draw light energy in to restore what she came to earth with and bring her back to her healthy, energetic state. Once she learned to balance her intake and outtake of energy, she fulfilled her urge to help others by taking some courses and soon opened a successful healing practice in Tampa, Florida. A benefit of healing for Cecilia is that, as she helps others, she also keeps her own energy balanced by not only putting out, but taking in when she works with her clients. I am happy to say her chronic pain is gone and she now lives a happy life with a new partner. Just as Cecilia suffered chronic pain, many physical illnesses can result from depleting your energetic body of light energy.

Combating Side Effects of the One-Way Flow

Balancing your energy and keeping it stable can be a simple thing if you understand what is happening. Aside from being drained of vital energy, I have seen one-way flowing Lightworkers suffer from various ailments that have been successfully treated or at least managed when they finally find their middle ground. Taking care of yourself is step one. Taking time to cleanse the chakras and open them up as receptors to light energy is something that should be done daily (see Chapter 4). You can do this with simple meditations, visualizations, or even by saying affirmations. Here is one simple technique you can practice to move energy both in and out of your body and help it flow evenly.

1. Each day, you must call on healthy energy and draw it into your body with visualization. Stand with your feet shoulder-width apart, close your eyes, and place your arms at your sides. Make sure no part of your body is touching (such as resting your hands on your thighs).

2. Visualize the energy that looks like white light coming into your body, drawing it up from the earth and from all around you. As you visualize this vibrant white energy entering your body, pay special attention to sensations you are feeling. You may feel a slight tingling throughout your body, as the energy comes into you. Notice if the tingling is more pronounced in a particular area. This could indicate that area in particular is being drained (for example, relationship issues/heart chakra).

3. In your mind, see the energy moving through your shoulders, down your arms, and into your hands. See the white light filling every part of your body like water filling a glass to the top. As you begin to fill up, you may also feel heat radiating from your palms.

4. When you feel "full," slowly open your eyes and shake your hands to shake off any excess that you do not need.

5. Call on the energy anytime you're feeling depleted or sluggish and you will feel revitalized and mindful of the light energy that you have absorbed.

Once you begin to consciously affirm that you are balanced and healthy, your energetic field will begin to react to what you're telling it. Here are some typical reactions to the one-way flow and some affirmation to begin working toward relief.

∞ Vertigo: I am centered and remain balanced in all I speak and practice.

∞ Lower back issues: My energy is focused and stable. I am aligned with my body and the earth. I belong and I stand connected.

∞ Colitis or irritable bowel syndrome: I will do what is right for me at this present moment in time without guilt or hesitation.

- ∞ Chronic pain syndrome (or unidentifiable pain): I feel only joy and contentment on my path to ascension. There is no pain and suffering within oneness.

- ∞ Fibromyalgia: I do not need to experience pain to be a healer here on earth.

- ∞ Weight gain: My emotions are my own and I am shielded from any harmful energy that surrounds me.

- ∞ Menstrual complications: I can take in and give out my light energy equitably and stay in perfect harmony with the energy of the universe.

- ∞ Infertility: My body functions in perfect balance and assists me in fulfilling my every desire while here on earth.

- ∞ Chronic Fatigue Syndrome: Each day I draw from the unconditional love of the Universe and I am entitled to boundless energy and vitality for life.

Of course there can be many organic causes for these conditions as well, but holistic and energetic healing can help alleviate some of the physical manifestations of energetic polarization. When we begin to focus on our physical ailments, we minimize our focus on our light energy and this creates a cycle of depletion as well. Obviously it is much better not to deplete or polarize to begin with so we don't have to go through finding our way out of the vicious cycle it creates.

Lightworkers and Darkworkers

Keeping in mind that everything in the universe has polarities, if we want to discuss Lightworkers, there must be a polar opposite. In order to keep balance in the universe, Lightworkers must have an opposite. A Lightworker commits to servitude to humanity and bringing light energy to the earth plane. Conversely, there are certain souls who do nothing but draw in the light energy, and give nothing back in return. Using the term Darkworker is not derogatory at all, because there is no concept of good and bad in the universe. Everything is contained within its oneness. Just as dark energy is neither bad nor evil, neither are those who practice Darkworking. Darkworking is the practice of taking energy or extracting light energy from anyone or anything with which you may come in contact. This is necessary to keep the energetic flow of the universe moving. But either giving all or taking all is creating a one-way flow and this is when we move from our balanced or centered point. Darkworkers believe that being takers will get them ahead and commit them to a life of only self-preservation and material gain. Does this make you a Darkworker if you commit to the servitude to your own happiness instead of others? Darkworkers are not evil (maybe predatory) unless they take energy through inflicting pain on others or creating fear to manipulate and give them power over others. Adolph Hitler may be the best example of an evil Darkworker. But a Darkworker isn't always evil, and it's really not so wrong to want to make your own self happy, but when energy is only flowing one way, (in the Darkworkers' case, inward), we are polarizing again.

Lightworkers who give away limitless light energy without taking in are the ones who fall into depression, become addicted, or even become enablers of Darkworkers. Remember, everything in the universe has a polar opposite, so we must have Darkworkers as well.

Just like the universe, we are comprised of every type of energy. Our energetic bodies are composed of both light and dark energy. It would be a mistake to dismiss the dark side of ourselves. Taking away the misconception that the darkness is evil is very important. It is impossible for the light to exist without the darkness. If we live with the assumption that dark energy is bad, we automatically begin to polarize our energy, because we as practicing Lightworkers, tend to want to shy away from what is dark. Evil does exist in the universe, but we have to separate darkness from evil. Evil is the result of dark energy being carried out with the intention of causing harm or pain to others. Dark energy alone does not cause harm without the evil intention behind it. Confusing dark energy with evil creates the impression that everything dark is evil. For example, we all feel sadness or grief at times during our lives. We could consider this a time when we are surrounded by darkness, but this doesn't make us evil. Its very difficult to integrate and accept the dark part of ourselves when we consider it to be evil, and this makes the ascension process more difficult. Refusing to accept a portion of yourself (and the universe for that matter) will not allow you to know your authentic self. Thinking you must be all light (or polarizing) is a slip up that will quickly become a drawback to your spiritual progress. Integrating both the light and dark is the most effective way to progress.

Embracing the part of you that is dark (however small that part may be) will help keep you balanced. To achieve oneness, we must accept every hue as our own and embrace the part of ourselves that takes as well as gives. A good example of a one-way flow is Lightworkers who practice psychic readings or spiritual counseling and refuse to charge for their services. When you have good intentions in your work and want to sincerely be of service to someone else, you should be compensated for your efforts in some way. Whatever exchange you decide upon will work as long as it's equitable. It can be payment in the form of money, or the exchange of favors or goods. This will create energy flow that goes two ways and keeps it all in perfect balance. Lightworkers who are not compensated for their services will quickly become depleted and their work will not be effective.

The fastest and most powerful way to ascension is to accept both sides, (the light and the dark) and embrace them both as fundamental parts of your whole and authentic self. When Lightworkers integrate both sides fully, they become truly powerful! Because our Source Creator is all things, complete oneness can only be achieved by the inclusion, integration, and acceptance of all sides of oneself and others without the foregone conclusions of good and bad or right and wrong. Lightworkers and Darkworkers are people who've chosen to polarize in their ascension path. But if you can practice centralizing your energy and successfully integrate both sides of the energetic forces of the universe, you will find the path to self-mastery.

6

Raising Your Energy and Vibration

Vibrations, frequency, and energetic flow all mean the same thing. As Lightworkers, there are times we feel trapped in our own vibration and confined by our humanness, but this is not necessary. You have worked hard to refine and raise the vibration of your energy to a fine-tuned frequency, but when you descended to earth, you may have begun to sing with the choir, and forgotten your own song. The earth plane has the lowest and slowest vibration of all the realms we will discuss and Lightworkers may begin to align with the energy of those around them, actually bringing themselves down a bit. You can purposely raise your vibration to align with the higher realms to visit for brief periods of time or perhaps live life at a higher frequency to integrate the gifts of the higher planes into our humanness.

First let's look at the seven planes and see what the gifts of each plane are:

∞ The 1st plane: Earth: This is where you now reside. The energy here is dense, heavy, and dark. You have come here to heal and share your enlightenment with humanity. This is where you take your human form.

∞ The 2nd Plane: The Astral Plane: This is the buffer zone between the earth plane and the higher planes of wisdom. You can astral travel here, meet with loved ones who have crossed over, and also confer with your spirit guides. Most of us travel there unintentionally during our sleep.

∞ The 3rd Plane: This is where you will master your gifts of intuition and need to embrace a higher purpose. Here you will begin to understand the difference between your physical self and your spiritual self. Here you understand the meaning of ascension and the desire to climb higher through the realms.

∞ The 4th Plane: This is where you master your gifts of sight and sound. All the beauty of the universe is here and you master the power of unity through creativity and healing through love.

∞ The 5th Plane: This is where you master enlightenment. All the information and knowledge of the universe is here.

∞ The 6th Plane: This is where you have mastered the gifts of all the realms and now have limitless powers. Your connection to your higher self is here.

∞ The 7th Plane: This is where you achieve oneness. Here you are united and in sync with all there is and your Source Creator.

As you ascend up the realms in frequency, you gain enlightenment and harmony in your life. You also gain knowledge and empowerment as you return to your original energetic state. Think of it as getting more of an aerial view, just as if you were in a plane looking down at the earth—you now see a bigger picture. When you're lower in vibrational frequency, you're grounded, and your vision is limited to only your line of sight. Also the lower your frequency, the more you are interacting with your ego or human self, which will limit the information you can receive in order to satisfy its fear-based beliefs. Raising your frequency is a task that incorporates body, mind, and soul, so you must be prepared to make some life changes. Right now, you have been functioning on a certain octave of vibration for most of your life; let's call it your soul melody. It is your note, your tune so to speak. Now it is time to change your tune.

Be and Emanate a Source of Love

There are many types of love that we can experience: love for our family, friends, and pets, and romantic love. Relationships that give us the feeling of love can be wonderful and create emotional bonds that can last, but the type of love that is healing is a shift from the sort of love we understand into a love that goes beyond the confines of your human side. Many times, the type of love we understand on a human, emotional level has fears and egocentric issues attached to it. They may be possessive or fear-based, and can actually work in direct contradiction of healing, unconditional love.

Whenever you connect human fear to any type of love, you run the risk of accumulating toxic energy in the heart chakra. In order to channel the healing type of love through the heart chakra, there must be no human attachments to it and human love must transform into universal love, which has no fear of loss or abandonment. In order to achieve this type of healing, universal love, we must first see our entire existence as an expression of love, as opposed to a feeling or emotion that comes and goes with people, places, and things in our lives. We must be in love with our existence, and see ourselves as our own source of love, first and foremost.

Make the conscious choice each day to release unconditional love to all creation through your heart chakra.

This is your primary work here as a Lightworker, so once you begin to incorporate the practice into your conscious mind, it is going to come naturally. Love is the most frequency-raising of all emotions, and the more you emanate unconditional love for yourself and others, the higher you will rise.

Be like water

Water is the purifying force of the earth. Connecting with water before your mediations or on a daily basis keeps your frequency flowing. If you're feeling stressed, taking a bath or shower will automatically raise your vibration. Simply being in the vicinity of a body of water will raise your vibration, so if you can find a large body of water near your home, visit it frequently. Your personal energy will automatically align with the flow of the water and you will find your life force moving through you at a more balanced pace.

Purify the body

Cut out unhealthy habits such as cigarettes, alcohol, and drugs. These habits are toxic to your system and toxins will weigh you down and make you feel sluggish. Pay special attention to your eating habits; thinking "light" in all you consume is a good rule of thumb. Heavy meat products and junk food only add to the garbage your endocrine system has to syphon out of your body. As we discussed, the lymphatic system and chakras work in correlation. Overloading your system with toxins will slow down your life force. A three-day juicing cleanse may be a good start. This will kick start your system and rid you of toxins. Of course, proper hydration is necessary. Please consult your doctor before attempting a juicing detox.

Practice meditation

Meditation is necessary for you to stay centered and grounded. It doesn't need to be a ritual or routine that takes you away from your busy day. But taking 10 or 15 minutes a day to connect with your higher-self and clear your energies is a must if you are going to live your life at a higher vibration.

Check your internal dialogue

Limit the mind chatter and keep it positive and uplifting. Pay special attention to how many self-deprecating comments you make each day and automatically correct yourself. When you catch yourself being negative or unkind to yourself, immediately envision the backspace button on your keyboard and erase it from your mind. Go back to the keyboard in your mind and envision different words, such as *There is nothing I cannot do!* or *I am loved and supported in all I do!* Keep the picture of those words in your mind for several seconds and then move on. As you begin to raise your vibration, your inner dialogue will automatically become more loving and kind, but until you get there, there is no need to keep dragging yourself down with negative self-talk.

Pay attention to signs and messages

Every day we are receiving divine messages and guidance from the universe. Spirit guides, guardian angels, and even loved ones who have crossed over are watching out for you all the time. The signs they send us are there, although many times we are so busy, we don't see them. Keep your awareness level raised by being open to the possibility that you are always being guided and you are never alone.

Connect with the gifts of the higher realms

Music, art, and literature are all gifts to humanity from the higher planes. Take time to connect with the beauty of these sources of higher perception. Just to lose yourself in the heavenly melodies of Mozart or the glorious colors of a Monet painting will raise your vibration. These works are a gift to us, they are meant to raise the vibration of the earth plane, and we should connect with their energy as much as possible.

Stay clear of negative people

People who gossip, lie, or are envious are of very low vibratory status. They are not enlightened and are material souls who believe only material possessions are of value and hold no importance of their spirituality. Be careful because these types like to reel others in with their fear-based conversations. They have a deep inner need to be liked and accepted, and because they lack spiritual enlightenment, they never feel worthy of love. They are not evil people, but they are misguided and their focus is on the illusion, not what is authentic. You are a Lightworker here to spread love and light and have no time for these types of people.

Work with crystals

Crystal therapy is a great way to raise your frequency. Meditate while holding a crystal and you will feel the vibrations emitted from it in your hands. Crystals are high vibrational stones with potent energy that can bring you to new heights. Certain types of crystals possess powerful healing energies and their frequency can be used to raise your own personal vibration. Crystals also resonate most strongly with the upper chakras (from the heart up) which is where Lightworkers do most of their work from. You will find yourself in perfect alignment with the crystals.

The quiet mind technique

The quiet mind technique will allow you to raise your vibration, clear your mind, and open up to "hear" the divine information that is meant for you. It is necessary to keep the mind in a calm, tranquil state when preparing to receive information from the higher realms during meditation. Follow this technique before you begin to tap into a higher frequency for answers or solutions. Choose a time and place when you are alone. Make sure all televisions, radios, and phones are off. Now is your time to connect with your higher-self.

1. Have a pen and paper handy for any messages that come through. Write them down as soon as you're done when they are fresh in your memory.

2. Relax the body; sit in a comfortable position and make sure your body is in alignment, your spine straight and your shoulders are back. Pay special attention to the chakras, making sure they are also aligned and unobstructed by your posture.

3. Breathing purposefully, concentrate on your breath as it goes in and out of your body. Envision breathing in pure light energy (picture it going in and out of your nostrils) and breathing out (through your mouth) whatever toxic energy that you have stored in your body. As you focus on your breath, know that you are being filled with life force that cleanses and energizes.

4. Listen intently; now is the time to begin to listen to the silence. As you open up your clairaudience, you will begin to hear the sounds of the universe. Begin to observe what you hear. Does it sound like the ocean, static, or music? Pay special attention to sudden flashes of images or single words. These are special messages that have meaning for you at this time and place.

5. If you feel your mind wander into the world of "What's for dinner tonight?" or "I need to make this deadline for work," pull yourself back immediately to the silence. This is about focusing yourself totally on the nonexistence of your human self. Within this quiet mind state, the ego and your perceived reality do not exist. Remember all that is material or physical is an illusion and aligning yourself with the energy of the earth plane will not move you along the ascension path.

This is all about expanding your consciousness outside the confines of your human self and reaching up to find a place of love, light, and wisdom that is not of this earth.

Part III

Healing With Love

7
The Power and Pain of Empathy

Empaths have the keen ability to perceive what others cannot through what they see and hear. Lightworkers' heightened sense of empathy is mastered on the fourth plane, (the plane of spirits who master beautification and intensified sensitivity to sight and sound) and Lightworkers who come directly from this plane incarnate to earth in order to work through their empathic skills. Because they are from the realm of sight and sound, they are highly sensitive to subtle inflections in someone's voice, or slight body movements or facial expressions that indicate underlying emotions. Being healers, they respond to what they are picking up and react to others in a soothing, healing approach.

Although all Lightworkers possess strong empathic feelings, fourth-plane spirits are more focused on empathy due to their position in their ascension path and the work they came to earth to do. The fourth plane is so rich in sight and tone that the human senses cannot process it. This makes empaths very sensitive to the beauty of art and music. Here the Lightworker discerns the differences between divine expression and the human manifestations of expression, and carries this knowledge here to earth to share it. This type of Light energy is apparent in the works of great masters of art such as Vincent Van Gogh, Leonardo da Vinci, or Rembrandt, where the use of colors, shadows, and overwhelming beauty seems to take us to other worlds when we set sight on it.

Fourth-plane Lightworkers' heightened sensitivity makes them highly responsive to what they see and hear around them. In fact, fourth-plane Lightworkers respond much more to what is going on outside than inside them. Many fourth-plane Lightworkers express their need for brotherly love and world peace through literature or music. Lightworkers John Lennon and Bob Marley promoted the message of peace and love for all humanity using music. Empaths such as this will seek to unite the world through the messages in their music.

Fourth Plane, Fourth Chakra

Fourth-plane empathic Lightworkers are associated with the fourth or heart chakra. The fourth chakra is where feelings of love emanate and fourth-plane empaths who are unaware of their authentic selves can easily begin to close the heart chakra and have relationship issues.

Carrie was a beautiful, successful, 25-year-old woman. She had a management position at an up-and-coming boutique and enjoyed living her passion as a fashion buyer. She came to me for spiritual guidance because she felt something lacking in her life. As we began her first session, I noticed what appeared to be a black, hazy spot in the area of her heart chakra, right in the center of her chest. As an intuitive, I can spot areas of trapped, toxic energy, and it appeared that her heart chakra was filled with this black, smoky substance. I also knew this was a sign of someone who endured some painful relationship issues and her heart chakra was closing fast. When I questioned her on this, she revealed to me that she endured horrible abuse at the hands of her first love. When she was 15, she fell in love with an older boy who took advantage of her and she had become pregnant. When the older boy abandoned her, she decided to terminate the pregnancy and was broken-hearted for a long time afterward. She told me that she had some therapy and felt she was over it.

It was clear to me that Carrie's issues were far from over and that she had closed her heart chakra long ago and trapped all the pain inside it when she was betrayed by someone she trusted. I explained that in order to move forward with healthy relationships, she needed to open up and clean out the heart chakra area. One suggestion was that she experience unconditional love as often as possible. By doing this, the heart chakra slowly and gently begins to open as unconditional love brings in the feeling of being safe and protected. I found one of the best ways to experience such a level of unconditional love is to work with animals or children. I noticed in my practice that those with the most heart chakra issues were drawn to working with animal rescue or children in need. Lightworkers will naturally gravitate to what they need to heal, and if they listen to their intuition, they will follow through accordingly. The healing love and acceptance that comes from working with these populations opens even the most wounded heart.

Carrie took a volunteer position at the animal shelter and began absorbing all the love she could. With each week, as she enjoyed her work, her heart chakra opened up more and more. We cleared out the toxic energy through guided cleansing exercises and soon romance flowed into her life as well.

~ ~ ~

Empathy Checklist

Read the following list and check those that relate to you in your life.

- ✷ *Strangers often approach you for assistance (asking for directions, asking for the correct time, and so on).*

- ✷ *You always seem to befriend or assist the new person (coworkers, people at social gatherings).*

- Friends and family always come to you with their problems.

- Compliments embarrass you or make you feel uncomfortable.

- You meditate better with music or you find listening to music very soothing.

- You are drawn to the arts.

- People say you have a friendly face.

- People say you are a good listener.

- People feel good after being around you.

- Many times you can tell what others are thinking just by the look on their faces.

If you checked more than five of these, you may have strong empathic sensitivities.

~ ~ ~

Relationship issues are also symptomatic of a highly empathic person who has not reached the awareness or mastery stage, because many empaths want to carry the burden of an entire relationship dynamic on their own back. Dysfunctional families, romantic relationships, and even work associations will more than likely have at least one empath in the mix trying to soothe everyone within the situation. What usually happens is the empath who is the "peacemaker" will usually become sick or depleted and end up with a total meltdown. But this is not something that has to happen; it can be avoided with the proper awareness and practices. If you feel you are an empath who is absorbing the pain of a dysfunctional relationship, consider the following:

∞ Do not blame yourself. Everyone has their own personal responsibility, even your adult children.

∞ Do not carry the guilt of the past. Holding on to what once occurred is not going to help anyone now.

∞ You cannot please everyone. People need to take responsibility for their own happiness; you cannot create it for them.

∞ Don't resort to martyrdom. Feeling as though you need to give all of yourself will not make the relationship equitable. This needs to be a two-way street.

∞ Know your place. Everyone has their zone within interpersonal relationships. If you feel out of that zone, you're not in the proper placement and the relationship has become unhealthy. Do not cross the boundaries into where others' accountabilities fall.

With the wave of fourth-plane Lightworkers entering the planet, we can actually see the physical symptomatic reactions within the population as well. Weight gain and morbid obesity numbers are at all-time high as are cardiovascular issues (effects on the heart chakra) as a result of stored toxic energy. Making our physical bodies sick is a tragic side effect of mismanaged empathy.

Managing Empathy

Being highly empathic is a gift and is also a major component that all spiritual healers must possess. At times, gifts from the Universe can be complex and hard to recognize, making it seem to be more of a hindrance in our lives instead of the spiritually restorative ability it is meant to be. The problems come about when highly empathic people are not aware that they have this ability and it then becomes a burden in their own lives. Imagine yourself as a mirror for all the people you come in contact with—all their responsibilities, problems, and emotional baggage. This could be overwhelming and create a whole assortment of meltdowns in people who are absorbing other people's energies and inadvertently taking them on as their own. Without proper understanding of their own gifts, eventually empathic people can begin to feel as though they are drowning in a sea of emotions as well as carrying the weight of the world on their shoulders. Once you have come to the understanding that you may be highly empathic (like many others) you will need to take steps to protect yourself and avoid the pitfalls, such as mood swings, addictions, chronic fatigue, and weight issues.

In order to avoid the pitfalls, an understanding of what qualities make you empathic is required. Empathic people are not only sensitive to energies, but profoundly reactive to sight and sound. They are natural healers with the acute ability to pick up the most subtle gestures or vocal inflections of others and instantly process them, recognize them, and generate a curative reaction. This all happens in an instant, never giving Empaths the time or opportunity to separate what they are taking in from their own emotional state. Day to day, this creates an energetic build up and a need to soothe their emotive polarities.

Constantly on a healing mission, telling empaths not to seek to heal everything around them is like telling a person not to breathe; it is simply an impossibility. So we must understand the main mission of the empath is a healing path. Empathy is a gift that must be held with extreme care. It is important that people who are undergoing empathic reactions do not become depleted and suffer side-effects that will inhibit their healing abilities, causing them to become energetically blocked and bring on undesirable effects, such as weight gain or relationship challenges.

The weight of the world

This is a healing gift that can sometimes be difficult to manage for the Lightworker who has not yet awakened or reached the mastery stage. When all the powerful emotions and influences come crashing down on them at once, the Lightworker can tailspin into feelings that are not theirs.

As a spiritual counselor, people come to me with all different life issues, from relationships, career paths, or health concerns that relate to heightened empathy. A new client once contacted me with concerns about her weight. As we discussed and analyzed the situation, it was evident to me she was highly empathic and a Lightworker descended from the fourth plane. I also observed that she was in phase 2 (negotiation, urging, and resisting) of her awakening process. Very often in my practice, I find one of the biggest challenges people with strong empathic abilities tend to have is weight issues that they just cannot correct with diet and exercise.

There are two main reasons weight gain is so common among empaths. The first one is energetic cushioning. This occurs when an empathic Lightworker instinctively seeks ways to protect their own aura or energetic field. This is common with empaths because of their strong response to what occurs outside their own energetic field; they unconsciously seek to soften or cushion the effects from the harsh energies that they experience from outside sources. Adding extra weight gives them the false sense that they are secure in this layer of dense mass that will keep their highly acute energetic field protected. This actually does no good at all and only creates more feelings of unworthiness and failure for the empath, which become a vicious cycle of seeking more relief.

Another reason for weight gain within the empathic individual is relief from the emotional states that can occur when they are acting as a mirror for those who are suffering around them. Continuously absorbing external energies of those who are suffering can create feelings of depression, lethargy, and any number of painful effects. Seeking out ways to sooth and quell the pain of others can result in indulging in comfort foods. These types of foods can work on a psychological level and induce temporary pleasure. Certain foods rekindle memories or sensations from the past (perhaps in childhood) when we felt safe and secure. We unknowingly seek out the feelings these foods give us to sooth the pain of being highly empathic. Also, there are other types of comfort foods that affect our mood by increasing the compounds in the brain used to manufacture the neurotransmitters, which give us a type of euphoria. Dieting doesn't work because this challenge is not a physical one at all.

Now that we understand the two main reasons empaths experience weight gain, next we will discuss more proactive and productive ways to combat weight gain and other undesirable effects of the wonderfully healing gift of empathy.

Creative outlets

One main quality of the person who possesses heightened empathy that is usually overlooked is their keen sense of sight and sound. Empaths are very sensitive to all things seen and perceived—hidden gestures, or tones or inflections of a voice. This also makes them very sensitive to all things of beauty and things that are not so attractive in the world. When empaths experience something of exquisite beauty, they feel a calming or a stirring that comes deep from within, something that is reminiscent of their soul's origin. Being so acutely aware (on a conscious or unconscious level) makes the empath want to create a world where only beauty may exist. As unrealistic as it seems, empaths do seek a nirvana here on earth and anything less brings on feelings of failure and sadness. Many great song writers, artists, and poets are highly empathic, and we see this not only in their work, but also in their painful lives and sometimes tragic endings. Wanting to live in a world that does not exist is literally painful to the sensitive spirit of the empath. As we discussed, energetic cushioning and comfort food are a way to soothe the pain of living in a world that is harsh when you are so complexly sensitive.

One way to alleviate the pain of dealing with the harsh earth plane is through creativity. History shows us that many empaths have taken the creative path to channel their gifts. Painting, writing, sculpting, and anything that is imaginative will help alleviate the pain and quell the need for cushioning or comfort foods. All Lightworkers of the fourth plane have creative talents that perhaps have been buried under experiences that occurred during the first phase of awakening (or childhood), and just the expression of creating will help relieve the strain of living in a world that is less than perfect. Because empaths are creative spirits who resonate with beauty on a deep soul level, it is best for them to release this tension by creating beauty. Any of the following activities can assist you in releasing empathic emotions.

∞ *Sculpting.*

∞ *Arranging flowers.*

∞ *Writing or journaling.*

∞ *Singing or listening to music.*

∞ *Dancing.*

Whatever outlets resonate with you personally will immediately bring you back to your main focus of beauty, expression, and functioning from the heart chakra. Creating beauty of sight and sound and sharing unconditional love is a big part of the highly empathic individual's soul purpose, and when that function is left stagnant, energies becomes blocked. These blocks create most of the painful consequences we have discussed here.

The empath is a natural healer. Many empathic people just naturally gravitate toward healing professions. A healing practice will assist in allowing empaths' energy to flow more freely. As empaths successfully center and ground their clients' energy, they will also automatically bring their own energy back to a healthy, flowing place. When working with clients during a healing session, empaths are also experiencing a healing or cleansing. If the empath is not properly grounded to perform healing, working with a client can bring on sciatica pain afterward as the root chakra struggles to connect to the earth plane and attempt to ground both the healer and the client.

There are all different healing modalities you can choose to practice (some thousands of years old), but energy healing has one main purpose: to become centered and grounded so that energy flows more freely. The phrase "healer, heal thyself" is befitting here; there are many benefits to people with heightened empathy becoming energy healers. You will not only be helping others, but you will also be helping yourself.

8
Your Most Sacred Conduit

When I began my work with unaware Lightworkers, I soon realized that many of them had relationship issues. They were either in dysfunctional or abusive relationships (either with friends, lovers, or family) or they seemed to never find a suitable partner. As my clients showed up in droves with these interpersonal issues, which in turn became feelings of being unworthy of love or unwanted, I began to wonder why the ability to connect with others was so challenging for them. Lightworkers are a unique prototype that is brought to earth to heal through the use of unconditional love, so why had so many of them become blocked off from the core of their healing resource, the heart chakra? I soon realized that it was for *that* very reason, because it *was* the core of their healing resource that the Lightworker's heart chakra was so vulnerable. I found that their first reaction to trauma of any kind was to protect what was most sacred to them—their portal for unconditional love.

Love Heals

The ability to feel compassion, sympathy, and gratitude, as well as to heal, are located within the heart chakra. This is also the chakra from which unconditional love emanates, which is the healing force of the universe. The main reason Lightworkers have come to earth is to heal by using this power. If the channel this power funnels through is blocked for any number of reasons, Lightworkers' power to heal is hindered and becomes disabled. We know that Lightworkers who are not serving their purpose (to heal) become lost and feel misplaced, creating many other problems that seem to spiral out of control, so special care and attention must be taken to ensure that your healing capacities are functioning. For Lightworkers, living a heart-centered life (or focusing our energy on loving compassion) is the most important practice because this is their purpose. Subtle techniques, such as being there for someone in a time of need, a prayer, or offering a hug to ease the pain of someone else are all parts of exercising their healing gifts.

Connects With Others

Your heart chakra is naturally associated with family, partners, friends, and animals. When it is clear, balanced, and open, you can touch others in a loving, healing way. Toxic energy can likely be stored here from traumatic events between the ages of 18–25, as the heart chakra is at its most vulnerable during this age range. I usually find that my clients will recount painful memories from this age bracket, but the heart chakra can become sick or can close up at any time. Situations such as divorce, separation, grief through death, emotional abuse, abandonment, and adultery create wounds that will affect our lives, relationships, and healing abilities if not healed. So it is important that, as a Lightworker, you keep the heart chakra balanced, healthy, and open.

To find out if your heart chakra is sick or if it is in danger or closing, ask yourself these questions:

∞ Am I dwelling on the pain of my past?

∞ Do I return over and over again to the same painful situations?

∞ Am I fearful of losing control of my emotions?

∞ Do I fear revealing my true feelings?

∞ Do I harbor guilt about past relationships or situations?

∞ Do I harbor bitterness or anger about past relationships?

∞ Do I feel I need to prove I am worthy of love?

∞ Do I fear rejection to the point of stopping myself from progressing forward?

∞ Do I find excuses not to make new friends, romances, or connections?

∞ Do I work so much I don't have time for my relationships?

∞ Do I suffer from asthma or breathing-related problems?

∞ Do I have high blood pressure or cardio vascular issues?

If you answered yes to the majority of these questions, your heart chakra may be in of need some healing. In my practice, I notice if clients' heart chakras are blocked or closed, they might have a tendency to shy away or avoid relationships.

My friend Joanne experienced some abusive relationships in her late teens and early 20s. She thought she had successfully moved past dysfunctional relationships when she left them behind and became engaged to Daniel who was a kind, giving, and loving man. The engagement was ongoing for six years and Daniel became impatient. He wanted to be married and start a family with Joanne, but she never seemed to want to talk about wedding plans, saying she was too busy with work, or maybe next year after she paid off her car. Daniel began to suspect Joanne was just stalling. Joanne began to turn cold and the relationship seemed to be at a dead end. Daniel began to feel used and mislead. Finally, after years of begging Joanne to marry him, he got tired of waiting and he gave up. Daniel left Joanne, and it didn't look like Joanne even cared. Daniel met and married Rita within a year.

Joanne and I talked about the situation and she asked me to perform a reading for her because she missed Daniel and was hurt that he left her. She wanted to know if she would find a new love, if would it be possible for Daniel to return, and what was ahead for her. Sadly, when I did her reading, it didn't look like any of what she wanted was going to happen. First, Daniel was never going to return. Second, I saw no love coming into her life and the underlying cause was that she was blocking it because of past pain and trauma. She thought just because she was able to move on to a "healthy" relationship, she had healed from the past. But what she did was manage to move forward with a closed heart chakra, consequently sabotaging her own happiness by not giving the relationship the nurturing it needed to survive. She had closed her heart chakra and it simply would not allow love to flow through it. Joanne might have intentionally pushed Daniel away (even though he was loving and kind) because she was now unable to feel a sense of connection. Her heart center had shut down completely. Her reading went on to indicate that by closing her heart chakra, she would continue to push people away, who in response would reject her (as Daniel eventually did when he left), seemingly validating her need for protection, and creating a vicious cycle of a self-fulfilling prophecy.

Above All Else, Love Your Self

Self-love is key for Lightworkers who seek mastery of their role, to fulfill their life purpose, and to advance on their ascension path. Without the practice of self-love, you cannot love others and you certainly cannot heal through love. Know that you are an extension of your Source Creator. The very same energy that fuels you can transform you. With this conscious awareness, you can begin to purposely shift thought and emotional patterns (correspondingly, your energy), from self-doubt to self-love. Just as you were brought here to heal others, you have the right to heal your own life. Acceptance of yourself and your soul path will also bring about self-love. Knowing that you are at this place and time for a reason and that your purpose for being is unique and important will help you to appreciate all that you have endured. With each painful experience comes soul growth. Growing pains are never easy, but if we love and nurture ourselves first, it makes it that much easier to heal.

Here is a five-step healing process that I give my clients. If you are able to implement these five simple words into your life, healing can take place very quickly, returning you to a place of self-love.

1. Experience (embrace the pain): To experience your pain is to own it and love yourself unconditionally (no guilt, fear, or worry) while going through it all, no matter how uncomfortable that feeling may be. The only way to release something is to first embrace it or own it.

2. Acceptance (consent that it has occurred): Denial is something that will keep you from healing. At times, the grieving process will take you through the stage of denial, but this only prolongs things. Acknowledging that the pain has occurred and cannot be undone is a step to healing it.

3. Understand (comprehend what it means to you): Look at the experience from all angles. Is this a life lesson? Part of your soul plan? Karma? Examining your experience and determining its purpose and what it means to you and your ascension plan will validate it instead of viewing it as just a random occurrence that has no potential to offer you spiritual growth.

4. Release (forgive and let it go): To finally clear the energy it has created in your spiritual and physical body, you must have forgiveness and gratitude for what you have learned and the blessings that come with the pain.

5. *Gratefulness (be thankful for the process)*: Have gratitude for the learning experience. Recognize the blessings that come with spiritual growth throughout the whole process.

This means feeling the pain of those emotions, and if we feel the pain of our emotions, then I suppose that means that we can't heal without first experiencing pain. So there really is no way around it. In order to transmute toxic energy locked in your heart chakra, you must experience it, embrace it, and feel love for it. These five simple words move you the through the healing process. Some words might take longer than others to penetrate into your energy, but once you reach the last stage of gratitude, you have healed your wound, released the toxic energy, and are now being flooded with healing light energy.

Keep the Heart Chakra Open and Flowing

The main goal is to keep the channel for love open and any source where you can find total and unconditional love is the place to seek it out. When I have a client who comes to me with a closed or blocked heart chakra, after some energy healing, my first suggestion is to visit an animal shelter. I know this may sound strange, but who gives more unconditional love than animals? Of course, if my clients have a pet, I suggest they spend some quality time with the animal. Here are some other easy ways to keep the heart chakra open and flowing:

∞ Work for charity: The energy exchange when you do this type of work is powerful. Volunteer work for a cause that resonates with you (children, animals, the homeless) will pull in the energy of loving compassion, which will flow freely through the heart charka.

∞ Do something kind for a stranger. Holding a door, smiling, or saying "Have a nice day" are simple things you can do to be a source of loving kindness to others. You will see strangers respond and the loving kindness will be reciprocated right back at you.

∞ Express your love for the people around you. Don't hold it in. If you love family members or friends, tell them so and often.

∞ Love and remember your inner child. Keep a photo of yourself as a child where you can see it often and this image will bring you back to a time when unconditional love was all you knew.

∞ Spend time with children. You can feel comfortable that you will never be judged or criticized by babies or young children. Babies will love you no matter how much weight you have gained or if your teeth aren't perfect. It doesn't matter; children are a pure source of love and joy. This is the time to bring out your inner child and just have some play time. Children will love and accept you as you are, unconditionally.

∞ Eat green foods. Green is a color associated with your heart chakra. Any vegetable that is a rich green color will keep the heart chakra happy and healthy.

∞ Do something you love and feel you're good at. If you have a special talent that you just never have time for, now is the time to exercise it. If you feel you have a knack for poetry, write some. If you love to paint, get out the canvas and begin a new painting. It's time to recall that part of you that is truly unique and gifted. Sometimes we forget to look at our abilities and the things we love about ourselves. Find time to cultivate and appreciate your talents and you will begin to re-member how wonderful you really are.

∞ Be grateful for all there is. Other than unconditional love, gratitude is one of the highest-level emotions you can live in. Being grateful for all the love and support the universe sends you each day will only open you up to more love. Make gratitude a state of mind and a way of life. Incorporate it into every aspect of your being and be grateful for each interaction, connection, and experience. Remember what we consider "problems" are just the universe bringing us the opportunity for spiritual progress, so be grateful.

Heart Chakra Affirmations

These affirmations will keep your heart chakra alert and at attention. Notice they all begin with "I." Keeping your heart chakra open is about self-love, first and foremost.

∞ I am comprised of eternal love.

∞ I am free of fear.

∞ I am released of any guilt I am carrying.

∞ I am loved eternally without conditions.

∞ I am a conduit for pure love and joy.

∞ I am deserving of happiness.

∞ I am entitled to balanced relationships.

∞ I am worthy of giving and receiving love.

∞ I am a conduit for the healing energy of the Universe.

∞ I am divinely guided.

∞ I am supported unconditionally by the universe in all I do.

∞ I am protected and shielded at all times.

∞ I am loved without limitations and boundaries.

Releasing Technique

We have all experienced heart pain in our lives. The problems arise when we do not process or release the pain properly. The more we hold on to it, the more it festers and becomes toxic within the heart charka, causing it to close up and block healthy energies of love and compassion.

There are many life changes and practices you can do to prevent the heart chakra from being harmed or closing all together, but if you feel it has already occurred, special healing techniques are necessary. Of course, it is a process that can take some time, but it is absolutely imperative that the healing process begin as soon as possible. The main purpose of these healing techniques is to release the pain (or toxic energy) stored in the heart chakra, allowing it to open and once again allow healthy energy to flow through it continuously.

The following process will help you release toxic energy by focusing on feelings within your physical body:

1. Sit comfortably and breathe into the moment as you become aware of each and every sensation in your body.

2. With each breath in and out, focus on what you're feeling. Do you feel pain, stiffness, or soreness in the area of your heart chakra? This uncomfortable sensation is toxic energy trying to release itself. Allow the uncomfortable feelings to continue. Do not attempt to stop or analyze this sensation.

3. Now, using visualization, turn these feelings into liquid form and allow them to flow out through the center of the chest. Allow it to pour out like a waterfall, cascading down and onto the earth below you. Stop this visualization when you feel it has emptied enough. Your body will let go of as much stored energy as it can at this time. Do not attempt to empty it out all in one session.

4. Thank the earth for absorbing this toxic energy and transforming it into light energy for the greatest good of all humanity.

5. Repeat this daily until you empty out the toxic energy and replace it with light, healthy energy. You will begin to feel a sense of lightness and well-being as you release and free your heart.

As a Lightworker, you are super sensitive and vulnerable to issues associated with the heart chakra. Unfortunately, if you do not heal or rid yourself of any toxic energy held there, manifestations of physical illness could result (see page 72 and diseases associated with the heart chakra). Body, mind, and spirit are all affected by the types of energy you allow to flow through you and that which you hold on to. In order to achieve mastery and alignment with your soul purpose, the heart chakra is the single-most important energy zone.

9
Attracting the Walking Wounded

The Well-Meaning Lightworker

Have you ever taken notice of the amount of needy people in your life? Many Lightworkers find themselves surrounded by them and often feel the need to turn off their phone or change their e-mail address! These people can be needy for any number of reasons, but mainly it is because they are wounded. These wounds are not commonly physical in nature, but spiritual and very deep-rooted. For any number of reasons, the "walking wounded" could be seeking out your healing energy as a way of finding comfort, dependency, and even power.

This is not just about taking advantage of your kind nature, but draining you of your vital light energy. Although being drained is an unpleasant experience, when a Lightworker meets up with the walking wounded, there is always the danger of developing a codependent relationship or one-way flow. The Lightworker has an inner urge to heal, and teaming up with the walking wounded isn't always the recipe for a win/win situation. A Lightworker's essential drive to want to "fix" who is broken often times infringes on their own happiness. Because a Lightworker is born with an innate ability to be of service to all of humanity, healing is something that comes quite naturally. Your tendency to attract the "walking wounded" or people in need of healing is something you will need to learn to accept as an intrinsic part of your nature and learn to master it. Here are some tools to aid in that process.

∞ Leave the heavy lifting to the Universe: There is something called Karma that resolves all issues and balances the scales perfectly. Cause and effect are happening all around us without you even realizing it. Karma is created by words, thoughts, and actions and if someone is hurting or heavily wounded, eventually it is going to balance out. It may not be before your eyes or even in this lifetime, but the Universe will make everything right.

∞ Become a more conscious observer: There is no need to get involved in everyone's issues and try to heal them. Instead, sit back and observe how people may be contributing to their own issues and how they may go about healing the situation. Instead of taking action, just observe and perhaps offer gentle advice on a solution.

∞ Release all judgments: Keep in mind not everyone would make the same choices you would. What is right for you and your path may not be right for someone else. Who are we to judge the path or Karma of another and try to change it? Try not to place judgment or your own priorities on others. They have their soul plane as well and there is a bigger picture that cannot be seen from the human conscious awareness.

∞ Do not refuse to accept darkness in others: Many people think that because they are Lightworkers, they must only see the good in all people. It is pretty hard to deny that there is darkness in the world. Refusing to accept that there are people who do not want to be healed or assisted will exhaust you! Accept the darkness. Do not judge it, but certainly do not deny it!

Who Are the Walking Wounded?

The walking wounded are those who live their lives with pain and trauma that they cannot or simply refuse to heal. They may harbor toxic energy in their chakra system, or even past-life trauma from which they have not recovered. As we go through our incarnation, we experience (through the natural course of living) unpleasant or painful events that leave us with voids, soul damage, or spiritual wounds. It's not that these individuals necessarily have had more pain or trauma in their lives than most, they simply don't learn from unfortunate circumstances and refuse to allow themselves to heal. They carry the festering wounds forever and taint every interaction they have with toxic energy. Many times these poor souls don't mean any harm, but don't know how to properly process their dark energy and become mired in it. Many times they seek out misguided methods of healing, such as substance abuse or consecutive bad relationships. None of this will work because the wounds are spiritual and only by expanding their own healing light energy will they heal.

Usually they will drain (if permitted) the Lightworker until the well is dry, sending the Lightworker into a perilous situation as well. This can bring on feelings of depression, worthlessness, fatigue, and physical illness.

Attracting wounded partners in relationships

Many Lightworkers seem to have a difficult time achieving happiness in relationships. Whether it is family, romantic, or even professional relationships, they tend to find themselves continuously on the short end of the relationship stick. They often feel doomed to live alone or without love, but in fact, aware Lightworkers who know how to create balanced energy exchanges seem to have the most long-lasting, thriving relationships of anyone. I find that many of my clients are involved with partners who have addictions or emotional issues, and even sometimes are in unhappy marriages with someone else. Lightworkers will try to find solutions and work to make these people happy, when in actuality, they are fighting a losing battle. These wounded partners take advantage of the Lightworkers with whom they are connecting.

My client Ted worked hard to get a prime management spot at a top resort hotel. When it came time to hire an assistant, Ted interviewed a slew of applicants. When Bernard, an unemployed concierge came in to apply, Ted felt an instant affinity toward him. He sympathized with Bernard because he was let go from his previous position and had a wife and kids. There were many other qualified applicants who were also out of work, but Ted was drawn to Bernard. He thought he was a nice guy who deserved a chance and he seemed motivated.

What Ted didn't realize is that Bernard was wounded by being let go at his prior job and was lacking self-confidence and the real skills to take on the job. Bernard played on Ted's sympathy, continuously mismanaged his position, and much of the work fell on Ted, who was anxious to impress the corporate big wigs. Bernard became a drain and Ted could not focus on his work with the thought of Bernard constantly screwing up. Ted soon realized that Bernard was not the man for the job, and, although he wanted to give him a chance, his mistakes were reflecting on Ted's work and his job was being jeopardized. With much regret, Ted let Bernard go and suffered anxiety and depression for weeks after.

We talked about the situation and through releasing techniques, I assisted Ted (who was aware of his Lightworker gifts) in releasing toxic guilt energy he had built up in his solar plexus from the situation. If Ted had thought about himself first and not the plight of an applicant off the street, he wouldn't have found his own job put at risk or suffered the guilt of having to fire a nice, but wounded man.

The same thing goes for romantic relationships. Many of my clients call themselves magnets for dysfunctional partners, and in a way they are! A Lightworker on a misguided mission to heal is like a loaded gun. Drawing the walking wounded into relationships on a conscious or subconscious level is a recipe for disaster. Many Lightworkers who are resistant to receiving give and give and don't know how or refuse to take in love and light energy, creating one-way flow and allowing their healing desires to go unbridled.

Becoming victimized by spirits

The walking wounded can also be in the spirit world. This involves spirits who are drawn to you for not only your light energy, but your ability to hear them, see them, or even enable them. You may not even be aware that you are interacting with these trapped souls, but you will definitely feel their effects on your life. Earthbound spirits are literally the walking dead of our earth plane and have no place here any longer. They are disincarnates who refuse (for any number of reasons) to move on to the spirit world, and find you comfortable to be around. They feel safe within your healing energy field, but they also drain you of vital light unless you are able to shield or detach from these lost souls. Spirits of lower vibratory frequencies and in extreme cases entities that have never been able to take human form can attach to you as well. Many times the profession that many Lightworkers end up in can lead to spirit attachment.

Lightworkers tend to gravitate toward the helping or service professions, working in hospitals or nursing homes where people often die. My client Monica worked many years as an aid in a nursing home and experienced a strange phenomenon one night. While working the overnight shift, 11 p.m. to 7 a.m., she found herself drifting off to sleep around 3 a.m.

It appears that between 3 a.m. and 4 a.m., astral travel is at its peak and spiritual activity in the physical world is more likely to occur because the veil between the physical and spirit world is considered at its thinnest.

As Monica struggled at not drifting off to sleep, she was startled when she heard a voice call out from the distance. She suddenly found herself standing up. She began to walk forward toward a narrow stairwell. She had worked at this nursing home for many years and knew this stairwell led to a patient annex that had been closed off several years ago. She followed the voices up the narrow stairway and when she arrived at the top of the stairs, she was amazed to see the darkened old ward still there. She walked the narrow hall, peered into rooms, and to her surprise there were patients occupying these rooms, only they were patients who had passed away years before. They were talking amongst each other, but not to her directly. She walked down the dark hallway, looking into each room, seeing once again the patients she used to care for. One woman by the name of Mary suddenly noticed Monica and called out to her. At that moment, with a jolt, Monica found herself back in her chair. She could see the narrow stairwell was boarded up once more and she no longer heard the idle chatter. The patients she had seen had not come back to life, but were still dead and attached to the nursing home they died in.

After that night, Monica began to experience strange sensations and visions. She was tired and feeling depressed. Concerned, she came to me for a consultation and during her first session I was able to dialogue with a spirit named Mary who was standing beside her. Upon hearing the name Mary, Monica understood and told me of her spine-chilling trip to this other dimension where the closed-off ward was. It was clear Mary had attached herself to Monica when Monica inadvertently entered the parallel world (or wing) that these earthbound spirits were now living in. After a few sessions, we were able to release Mary into the light and free her from the attachment to Monica and the deserted, dark wing. Sadly I could not reach the others and as far as I know, their souls remained in the darkened quarters of the closed off ward.

It's apparent the environments you enter, work, or live in can put you at risk. A Lightworker can invite attachments in places where maladapted or malevolent spirits congregate, such as bars or pubs. Many times spirits of the alcohol-addicted will hang around just waiting to attach to someone who can help enable their addiction by attempting to live vicariously through the patron who enters to drink. Once again, shielding is just as important as wearing a seat belt. Do it as a precaution wherever you go because needy spirits could be found anywhere. Simply envision yourself surrounded by a white light that looks somewhat like a bubble. Make sure you envision the light going over your head and under your feet. This psychic shield will protect you from others who draw your energy as well. Do this several times a day if you feel it's needed.

It may be all in the plan

At times, the wounded have already worked their trauma into their soul's plan. They may have contracted this event before even being born, but have forgotten their contract. Certain painful situations are placed in a life path purposely to promote spiritual growth, Karma, or even light energy expansion. In this case, the wounded must rise above the circumstances and learn from what has caused them pain. Under these circumstances, a Lightworker may actually interfere with the soul growth of another person. We can assist or promote growth by counseling or supporting the person, but there are certain occasions that we are not meant to "fix" someone. In these types of situations, we can do more harm than good.

You can decipher a soul plan from happenstance by the actions of the person. When a person is absolutely set on a certain road, or is clinging to a certain attachment, situation, or existence, it indicates that it is part of that person's soul plan. He or she will show an unquestionable resistance to being diverted from this position and this clearly shows he or she is not to be interfered with.

Part IV

Answers From the Universe

10
The Illusion of Time

Because the universe is complete, past, present and future all co-exist harmoniously. The past and the future were created to measure the human understanding of life. In reality, universal time is always in the present—all things happening at once, together. Are there ways to combine the past, present, and future to create an improved "now" experience? In order to stay on the Lightworker course, you need to understand the meaning of being now-oriented. A Lightworker who is not focused in the present becomes trapped and fearful. Within the universe, there really is no time. It is in the now where you can shape your purpose and bring yourself to your fullest potential. By mixing the best of all three zones, we are our most empowered selves.

Being present is not as easy as it seems, because we tend to develop behavior patterns that either recreate the past or create obstacles for our future. You will find if you're stuck in the past—either nostalgia for the good old days or carrying the pain or trauma from events gone by—you will become trapped and unable to move forward. Conversely, if you are too future-oriented, you will find that you will form attachments to certain outcomes which may not suit you when you eventually reach your destination. Living in the now is an empowering way to create your existence and allows you to feel secure knowing what is ongoing; of course if you're in the present time, there are no uncertainties or fears of what is to be.

My client Jillian was going through a major life challenge. Her eldest son Brad contracted a life-threatening condition and because Jillian's children meant more to her than life itself, naturally she was having a difficult time living with the idea of possibly losing her son. As I counseled her through each and every part of her son's illness, we worked at staying in the present, where her son Brad was present, fighting his illness and still very much alive. This brought her comfort to know Brad was with us and thriving, without wandering off into the uncertainty of the future. This held Jillian over throughout each hurdle of her son's illness until his recovery. I am happy to report that Brad's condition is in remission and he is living an active life, and Jillian is still focusing on the now and not drifting off into the past where Brad was sick or the future and the fears of a relapse. There is no need for Jillian to go back into the painful experience. This experience ceases to exist except in Jillian's memory (or conscious awareness) and certainly there is no need for her to travel into the future and into the slight chance that Brad may be sick again. Staying in the now keeps her safe, secure, and happy.

Soul Fragmentation and Soul Retrieval

When we experience painful or traumatic events, a condition called soul fragmentation can occur. We have all heard the expression, "When he left, he took a piece of me with him" or "What happened just broke my heart." These expressions are not literal or referring to your physical body, but your spiritual body. There is real meaning behind these phrases and we can literally become broken or fragmented spiritually when we experience pain or trauma.

The goal is to retrieve the missing fragments (or shards) of our soul to become whole once more. There is a process called Soul Retrieval where one must mentally go back in time and retrieve the missing shards. Soul Retrieval is the recovery of soul fragments that have been left or lost somewhere, or that were stolen or borrowed by somebody else. The objective is to make the person whole and more present.

It is amazing where my clients find their shards. Some may find them in the pockets of people they once knew;

others may locate a shard in a cupboard of their childhood home. First and foremost, you must identify what is truly missing. Certain expressions can help you identify your missing shard. If you use any of the following expressions, it may be an indicator of what you need to retrieve.

∞ *I lost my innocence when that happened.*

∞ *He took a piece of my heart.*

∞ *I don't have the strength I had when I was 20.*

∞ *He robbed me of my dignity.*

∞ *She took away any hope I once had.*

∞ *They took away my authority.*

∞ *My father robbed me of my self-esteem.*

∞ *He took my childhood from me.*

∞ *That home holds all my happy memories.*

∞ *My sense of security went out the window.*

You get the idea. So listen carefully to the expressions you use and this will give you many clues as to what you need to retrieve and from who or where. Your shard is out there, waiting to fit into the missing slot. Like a shattered mirror, by replacing the missing pieces, Soul Retrieval will assist in seeing your true self and being whole in the present.

Soul Retrieval originates in ancient shamanic practices. American Indians would practice this in drumming ceremonies where the shaman would travel off into the past and find the part of the person that was missing and bring it back into the present. You don't need a shaman to practice Soul Retrieval; you can do it yourself quite simply.

Here is an easy Soul Retrieval method you can try yourself. This is like a journey with your higher-self through time. I highly recommended that before attempting this, you have balanced and cleansed your chakras (see chakra meditation on page 78) within the last day or two. This will ensure you have a clean aura that will not release any toxic energy as you complete the following journey. Have a pen and paper next to you to write down any impressions or messages you received when you emerge from this journey.

Prepare for your journey through time by lying down in a comfortable position. It is very likely you will fall asleep at the end or during this process. Falling asleep is fine, once you set out on this journey. Even if you fall asleep before you find your missing shard, your higher-self will continue to search as your consciousness rests.

1. As you settle in and begin your conscious breathing technique, visualize your soul leaving your physical body behind. As you begin to move forward, you will envision the indigo door to your higher-self. It glows brightly and as you turn the knob to enter, state your intention. For example, "I wish to find my ability to trust again" and know that the trust you lost long ago is on the other side of this indigo door somewhere.

Enter and know that you are now on a mission to find this missing piece of yourself.

2. As you enter, you will find your tour guide on this journey—your higher self. Your higher-self welcomes you with an embrace. Your higher-self will hand you an empty white bag. Accept the bag as the two of you set out on the sacred path of retrieval.

3. In front of you is the sacred path of retrieval. Take note of the path. What does it look like? What is the surface of the path made of?

4. Noting your surroundings, what do you see? What is around the path? What are you wearing? What is the weather like? Everyone has a different sacred path, so pay attention to yours. It says a lot about who you are and what is important to you.

5. As you and your higher-self walk your sacred path, you will soon come to a large mansion. This is your inner castle, where you keep all your worries, fears, treasures, joys, and experiences within. As you approach your inner castle together, look at it as you get close. What does it look like? What color is it? What is it built from? Are there trees and flowers or is it barren? Again, this will be highly specific to you. Pay attention to everything. Note every detail.

6. Enter your inner castle with the mission of carrying out the intention you set in the beginning. Explore

everything. You can talk to yourself here. You can talk to your higher-self about issues that are troubling you. Look into the rooms. Do they look familiar (perhaps like your childhood home, or a place you once worked)? Is there anyone in the castle? Who are they and what are they doing there?

7. Continue to search each room in your castle until you hear a "recall" sound (a distinctive change in the pattern of vibration or pitch in volume). This is your shard calling to you. Follow the recall until it gets louder and more intense.

8. Once you locate your shard, retrieve it. Take special note of where it was found or if there was anyone there in the room. This will indicate the time and place in your life where you experienced the loss. Place the shard in your white bag.

9. Walk back down the path with your higher-self, and know that you have retrieved what was once lost and you are now whole.

10. As your higher-self guides you back to the indigo door, embrace and express gratitude to your higher-self for being your guide throughout this journey. Exit through the indigo door. Your mission is now complete.

11. Breathe back into your physical body and open your eyes slowly. Now is the time to write down all the details of your journey for further examination.

Many people can easily recall during meditation or even self-hypnosis where their shard may be. Perhaps 10 years ago you felt on top of the world, but after a string of painful events, you lost all your self-esteem and confidence. Soul Retrieval allows you to go into the past and identify the people and situations that contributed to your loss and take back the missing pieces just by allowing yourself to take a mental journey through time.

Being Too Forward Thinking

We tend to want to be more, or feel we should be doing more than we are currently, holding ourselves to the ideals of others or comparisons to others. But in actuality, we are doing exactly as we should be. Understanding that everything occurs in divine timing will allow you to accept where you are currently and move forward from that point. Taking the pressure off of what the future holds is an empowering feeling. Imagine living each day with the knowledge that you are exactly where you should be at any given moment. As we move into the future feeling now-oriented and with ultimate faith, we begin to feel filled with promise and relieved to know that the future is now, occurring as you read this sentence!

Future-Life Progression

FLP or Waking Dream Therapy is like stepping into the future and getting all the wisdom of an experience that is yet to come. It is a therapeutic technique in which information from your future life is revealed, reviewed, and integrated into the present. You can also sample alternate futures, or play out different outcomes to future situations which will enable you to make decisions with the benefit of foresight. FLP allows you to see into your future—you can envision your relationships, career, or health path, the place you live in, or anything that you choose to focus on during your time travel. Understanding that the past, present, and future exist in the same now experience helps you comprehend how you can access all the possibilities of what is to come in your life. Because all events are ongoing, it's kind of like remembering; remembering the future that is.

You can practice FLP with the help of a hypnotist or learn techniques to do it yourself, but in my experiences with clients, it does occur spontaneously or unprompted sometimes. You just need to have an awareness it's happening. We can recognize this kind of FLP when we repeatedly dream of a situation we have never been in, are drawn to particular names, or develop a certain attachment to a place or person for reasons that seem to make no sense for you.

For years, my client Joann began hearing the name Michael Anthony. It started when she was just 14. There was a young boy she had a crush on by that name, but as she became an adult, she would see the name on store fronts, street signs, and sometimes even in the phone book. She would think, "Well, it's a common name, but there it is again." She began to really take notice one day when she saw the name while browsing an Internet dating site she had joined a year earlier. "Oh but this Michael lives 1,500 miles away in Florida," she thought. There would be no chance to meet or have a relationship with this Michael Anthony. She wrote it off as a weird coincidence. Two weeks later, she received a note in her inbox from Michael Anthony of Florida! Turns out he felt drawn to her profile and even though she was "geographically undesirable" he thought, "What's the harm in making a new friend?" and messaged her. It didn't take long before Joann was packing up and moving to Florida to be with her fiancé Michael. Never forgetting how she always seemed to come across the name, she now understood the connection.

Placing the Future in the Present

Another way of planning for the future in the now without feeling pressured is to create a vision board: Using a vision board to attract the future you desire is one way of staying now-oriented and still working on your manifestation for the future. A vision board is simply a visual representation of the things that you want to have, be, or do in your life. It consists of poster or cork board where you can tack or tape images of your goals. The purpose of this is to create a pictorial to set into motion the energies that will actually draw these things into your life. If you would like a stable, happy relationship, you may want to clip a magazine image to represent that, such as two lovers strolling on the beach. If your goal is to lose weight, perhaps you can find an image of a person who is of ideal weight and glows in the peak of health. All these images will activate the law of attraction as you begin to move forward, carrying these images in your mind and manifesting them into your life.

In today's day and age, we are too distracted by time and how the past and future distorts our reality of the present moment. Imagine we had no concept of time and how that would change your entire perspective on life. We would seize the moment more often, live for the day, and not stress about what is to come. If we all lived on universal time, it would even alleviate our fear of death! Of course, this is not entirely possible when we all have schedules and deadlines, but if we would just allow ourselves to stay conscious of the present moment, it will alleviate the pressures associated with the concept of time.

Now that we understand that time is an illusion and all things happen concurrently within the universe, let's look at how we can access answers and solutions at our will through dreams and other tools that can guide us.

11
Dreams: The Doorway
to the Universe

Freud described the subconscious as just below the level of the conscious mind and containing thoughts and feelings that a person is not currently aware of, but can easily be brought to consciousness. Traumatic emotional experiences may be in the subconscious as it waits to problem-solve during dreamtime. But is the subconscious mind that Freud theorized really just the guardian of the sleep state or could it also be the gatekeeper to the universe? Aside from being a proficient problem-solver, the subconscious can also act as the doorway to other realms that bring us knowledge, guidance, and enlightenment.

In 1969, my mother had been hard at work on her metaphysics training, which included healing work, psychic readings, and meditations for guidance and direction. It was in February when she began to experience a repetitive and disturbing dream. In her dream, she recalled running down a dark street. The street had a sheen to it, like it would look after rain. The night felt cold and damp. She ran down the endless pavement crying and screaming, "My brother is dead, my brother is dead!"

She would awaken, shaking and with her heart pounding as if this was really happening. She wondered which brother, because she had two and she could not shake the eerie feeling that something bad was going to happen. At times, she dreaded going to sleep and having the dream again. She asked in meditations for more details, but no answers came. Eventually, the dreams stopped and she felt relief that they were gone. Both brothers were young and healthy, so she tried to put it out of her head.

Then in the summer, tragedy struck when her youngest brother Joey drowned at the lake where he had been working. The day my mother got the news, her cousin drove her to the lake to be with Joey, whose body still lay on the beach. As they drove, it was twilight and a light drizzle fell on the streets, reminding her of the dream. After this happened, my mother became resentful and was angry that her spirit guides didn't provide more information so she could save her brother. In fact, she was so angry that she stopped her training for the next year and refused to speak to her guides. But did this information come from her spirit guides, or are all the answers there for us to access on our own?

Lucid Dreaming

What my mother experienced was a prophetic dream and she entered into a dimension where future events can be accessed. This leads us to wonder: If all events are happening concurrently and there is only "now" in the universe, perhaps if she had asked the right questions or took action in her dream, would she have been able to save her brother? This concept says the future is out there, happening as we speak; we just need to know where this information exists and how to go out in search of it.

An important part of accessing the information is remaining in control and consciously present in your dreams. A lucid dream, in simplest terms, is a dream in which one is aware that one is dreaming. The term was coined by the Dutch psychiatrist and writer Frederik van Eeden. Have you ever been frightened during a nightmare, and said to yourself "This is only a dream"? If you have, you have experienced lucid dreaming. A lucid dream is a conscious process in which the dreamer may be able to exert some degree of control over what is happening within the dream. Lucid dreaming allows dreamers to govern what they do, ask, or maybe even change the outcome within the dream on a conscious level.

Going with the concept that all events are happening concurrently in the universe and somehow we are led to the future with a prophetic dream, can we change the future with lucid dreaming?

Molly was a loving mother to four active daughters between the ages of 6 and 14. She was not exactly over-protective, but she kept a loving watch over her daughters as they went about their busy and varied routines. One night, Molly dreamt that her youngest daughter (6-year-old Meagan) did not return home from school. In her dream she set out on a frantic search for Meagan. The school yard was empty and desolate, and in her dream, darkness began to fall as she searched to no avail for her daughter. She awoke with tears streaming down her face and a feeling of panic that she had never felt before in her life. The next night, the dream returned, and again Molly awoke in tears with the same horrifying feeling. On the third night, Molly began to dread sleep, but she thought if this dream returned she would not awaken until she found Meagan. Sure enough, the same scenario in her dream oc-curred, but this time Molly pushed through. She knew she would not leave that school yard (or her dream) without her daughter. In her dream she searched, determined to find Meagan, and finally located her curled up under the sliding pond in the school yard. She held her daughter tightly in her dream and this time woke up with tears of joy streaming down her face. Molly was relieved that the terrifying dream did not return after this.

Two months later, Molly received a notice from the school that there was a child predator in the area trying to lure children into his car. The memo issued a warning to both parents and students that there was a man in a green Pontiac who had attempted to abduct an 8-year-old girl who was walking home. Molly recalled her dream and shuttered as she wondered if this could have been Meagan (who walks that same route home each day). For the rest of the school year, although it was only a short distance, Molly picked the girls up from school just to be on the safe side, but she wondered if her dream was a warning to her and if she had not persisted in finding Meagan, if perhaps her daughter would have been abducted.

Guidelines to lucid dreaming

∞ Pay attention to what is happening in your dreams.

∞ Work on remembering your dreams.

∞ Keep a dream journal.

∞ Raise your awareness level during waking hours (pay attention to what is happening in your life that may have a connection to your dreams).

∞ Link your conscious awareness to your dreams and prepare to take action in your dreams based on what is happening in your life.

∞ Prepare for lucid dreaming by telling yourself what you want to accomplish in your dream before sleep. (Molly telling herself she would not awaken until she found Meagan.)

Dream Doorways

Because everything is contained within the universe, it is possible that we can summon information, solutions, power, and wisdom through our dreams. If we think of the subconscious as the gatekeeper to the universe and all the answers are out there, we just need to find the entranceways and enter through. We will envision seven different doors; each door will represent different information and solutions we may seek out. Each door looks different and will lead us to whatever we are in search of. We can find these doors whenever we alter our state of consciousness, whether we are meditating, daydreaming, or in full sleep mode. Once we establish the pathway to these doors, we are always free to enter through them when needed.

Dream door number 1: The red door to will and empowerment

Through this red door, you will find an endless supply of positivity, strength, and willpower. Your strength and gift of free will and control are through this door. It is the door to your inner power. When you enter this door, you find your inner strength and the will to overcome any situation. Use this door anytime you feel defenseless. You will awaken with renewed strength and answers to the questions for resolving situations in which you feel immobilized. Use this door when you need courage, diligence, quick discernment, leadership abilities, persistence, and resolution.

Enter this door when you seek:

∞ To overcome addictions.

∞ Escape abusive relationships.

∞ Release from a undesirable work situation.

∞ To overcome chronic health issues.

Dream door number 2: The orange door to love and wisdom

Use this door when you need to be connected to unconditional love and the source of your divine intuition. Through this door, you will find the gateway of the loving place that is the oneness of any group or life situation; use this door when you need to see beyond the difference of others and seek answers to resolving conflict. Ask for resolutions to issues that involve relationships or conflicts with others here.

Enter this door when you seek:

∞ Tolerance.

∞ Open-mindedness to other people's ideas.

∞ To resolve conflicts in personal relationships.

∞ A solution to the inability to work with coworkers.

∞ To find forgiveness.

Dream door number 3: The yellow door to intuition and spiritual connection

Through this door you can connect with the spirit world. You can connect here with anyone you wish. You can visit with deceased loved ones, meet with spirit guides, and call upon those you wish to connect with who are alive as well. Also, your powers of extra sensory perceptions and prophetic dreams come through this doorway.

Enter this door when you seek:

∞ *A visit with a deceased loved one.*

∞ *A meeting or consultation with spirit guides.*

∞ *Information on future events.*

∞ *Connection with another person.*

∞ *Access to your extra sensory perceptions.*

Dream door number 4: The green door to unity through creative expression

This is the door to the gifts of creative expression in all forms. It is the door through which you will find harmony through inspired imagination. Here you will find your power of expression of beauty and sound. Your inner healer can also be found here to assist you in healing yourself and others.

Enter this door when you seek:

∞ *Empathy.*

∞ *Creativity.*

∞　Healing abilities.

∞　Sympathy.

Dream door number 5: The blue door to manifestation and divine intelligence

This door is the gateway to source intelligence. Here you can log into the ethereal hard drive and extract any information that is needed. It is all-knowing and complete, and all answers to the questions of life can be found beyond this doorway. Source intelligence ready to be used in service to humanity and manifestation in all ways can be accessed here. Anytime you are thinking outside the box, looking for unconventional solutions, or need to clear the path to your goals, answers can be found here.

Enter this door when you seek:

∞　Adaptability.

∞　Clear intellect.

∞　Clear communication.

∞　To develop a clear plan of action.

∞　To be more detail-oriented.

Dream door number 6: The indigo door to the higher-self

Here you can connect with your true essence, your spiritual self. This is where your authentic self resides as opposed to the fear-based human conception of yourself.

Here you will find the answers to where you came from, your soul's plan, and what your purpose is. Fear and ego are stripped away and you are comprised of only love and divine wisdom.

Enter this door when you seek:

∞   *To discover your soul's plan.*

∞   *To discover the spiritual nature of an illness.*

∞   *Freedom from fear-based behavior patterns.*

∞   *Clarification on your emotions and feelings.*

∞   *Answers about your life purpose.*

Dream door number 7: The white door to oneness

Here is where you will merge with the universe. It is a place of complete and ultimate peace and harmony, love, light, and divine wisdom. You will come here when you wish to go beyond the confines of the "self" identity and are in sync with your Source Creator.

Enter this door when you seek:

∞   *Unconditional love.*

∞   *To commune with God.*

∞   *To escape from artificial boundaries of humanity.*

∞   *Enlightenment.*

∞   *To just be.*

Dream door meditation

Once you find the pathway to your doors, you will easily be able to access them at will. But until you forge this pathway, you may need to go into meditation to locate the door you are in search of. Practice this meditation to find your doorways:

1. Sit or lay in the most comfortable position possible because you will most likely fall asleep during or at the end of this meditation. If you intend to do this before bed, do this meditation in bed. Shut off all televisions or radios. It is important to use the quiet mind techniques we discuss on page 102. Begin to breathe in and out at a steady pace and relax into each breath as you go deeper into the quiet mind state.

2. Picture a pathway that leads to a beautiful house, surrounded by green landscaping and beautiful flowers. This house can look anyway you like, because this represents entering your own subconscious. As you walk the pathway to the house, you know exactly why you are there and what answers you seek. You understand that all answers are there for you as you enter.

3. As you approach the main doorway, you turn the doorknob and it opens up effortlessly for you. As you enter, there is a welcoming feeling and you feel at home. Notice the interior and how it is furnished; this will be different for everyone.

4. You will approach a staircase and you will ascend the staircase until you reach the top. At the top of the

staircase, you will find seven doors along a long corridor. You notice each door looks different and is a different color. State your intention for being there.

5. Walk along the corridor until you find the door you seek which coincides with your query or the issue you need to resolve. If you do not have a specific question, let the universe be your guide and lead you to the door you need to enter.

6. As you turn the door knob to open your door, again state your intention and what you seek to know. (I seek know how to resolve my issue with ___, or, I seek to know why I am sick with ___.)

7. As you enter through the door:

    ∞ Know that the answers are there.

    ∞ Observe what you see (people, images, or scenes).

    ∞ Observe what you hear (one-word messages, songs, or noises).

    ∞ Pay attention to what you are feeling (cold, lonely, or sad).

    ∞ Note your observations because they will give you the answers you are seeking.

8. If you fall asleep, pay particular attention to your dreams and write the information in your dream journal for future reference. The answers will come, but remember to quiet the mind because any mental chatter will interfere with the clear messages that await you when you enter the gateway to the universe.

12
Tools That Guide

Destiny vs. Free Will

Many people feel that we are set on a course and destined to travel that road no matter what we do. Others believe that we have free will to change the course of our lives or choose to take a turn that will lead us in a totally different direction. I tend to believe it is a lot of both. When we are ready to incarnate, we make a plan. We create this plan with our teachers and guides who are there to assist us in our ascension path. All our lessons are incorporated into this plan; all the good work we intend to do, and things we wish to accomplish in this lifetime are all in this plan. The soul's plan sets up the map and when we incarnate, we have every intention of following it. That would be our plan or our map—our destiny. But when we incarnate, we must also interact with the plans and destiny of others and the grand scheme of life can be shifted sometimes, taking us off our planned path. Without directions, we can get lost. But we are not without assistance.

Because Lightworkers have this inherent ability to see the bigger picture or the aerial view, it makes sense to allow yourself some guidance to avoid some bumps in the road. These inherent gifts were earned and are yours to guide, you so you can stay on course during your incarnation. Being able to peek into the future will allow you to see the best path or path of least resistance to your goals. Tools have been used for thousands of years to help pull in the answers that are already there down the road. If we believe the idea that time is an illusion and all things are happening concurrently, then the future doesn't fit into the equation.

Divination Tools

Divination is the ability to foresee the future and discover paths of least resistance to your goals. Divination can also include seeing the past and present, and can help put ongoing concerns in proper prospective, give an objective view point, and help you find practical solutions. Because Lightworkers are super sensitive and have highly acute extra sensory perceptions, it is a very normal occurrence for them to get psychic impressions or experience premonitions. You will find the more you open up to your role, the more you will experience glimpses of the future. The higher your vibration is, the more you are able to see.

It's like getting an aerial view from a plane—suddenly you can see all the streets and where they lead. But if you are grounded (or have a low vibration) you can only see what's directly in front of you. Some people have no interest in knowing what lies ahead. They wish to allow destiny to take its course and not interfere with it. This is fine too, but it can be helpful to know if the road you're on is a dead-end, or if your traveling down a one-way street.

We all have extra sensory perceptions, and Lightworkers, being so super sensitive, have highly acute ESP. They are much more aware of energies and can decipher information from sources that we cannot see with our eyes. All Lightworkers receive this information spontaneously, but many do not trust their intuition or become attached to preconceived beliefs that will reject the information coming in. When we use tools, we tend to trust the information because it is tangible, and we can actually see the information coming in. But in reality, we are the ones drawing the information into the tool. It's just that sometimes our human side tells us we need to see it to believe it.

Lightworkers do have this natural ability, but a tool or instrument can help you focus your energy and really clarify your psychic impressions. You can learn to do it for yourself or others with the intention of bringing divine guidance, wisdom, and even practical guidance to their lives. Because we understand that the universe is complete and there is no concept of time, we also can conclude that all things are ongoing and we can get a glimpse of the road ahead. It will give us some insight into what the road has in store for us using many different methods, and these tools can come in very handy when you need some direction. By using these tools, we can be prepared for obstacles or blocks along our path and find ways around them.

I want to make it clear that these tools we will discuss may be thousands of years old, but are really just instruments to implement your own divine gifts. Your connection to the universe and source intelligence is where the information comes from, not a set of cards or handful of stones.

Having the proper mindset

When using these tools, keeping a clear and objective state of mind is important. The answers are being pulled from what I call the "ethereal hard drive" where all information is stored in the universe for all eternity; all things past, present, and future are stored there and like a giant, non-corruptible computer, you can log in and extract the information you need.

If you attempt to read for yourself using one of these tools, it is very possible your wishes and desires may come through instead of a clear answer. Many times psychics will also have hopes that their clients will get what they wish for and taint the answers they get from the tools. Remember, you control these tools; the answers are being channeled through you, not the tool. Allowing your own partialities and attachments to interfere with the tool defeats the purpose and you will garner absolutely no value from the tool whatsoever.

Make sure you have a specific question. Asking for general readings, as in, "What is going to happen this year?" is not ideal. The answer can be very vague and may be difficult to interrupt. You need to focus in on something specific and channel the information that pertains to one question at a time.

It is also important to believe in your intentions. If you believe that your life is completely dictated by fate and that only the cards or the stars can guide you, you are mistaken. We all have free will, and can change our "fates" any time. Most of us, however, go with the "line of least resistance" in our lives, and continue to follow along with the natural flow of things without resistance. Oddly enough, this is partly why psychics are able to predict future likelihoods. I use the word "likelihoods" because that is exactly what each reading is. Not a scenario cast in stone, not a certainty, not an absolute. With free will, you can change any likelihood you see, and thus change your "fate" (and the outcome of the reading as well). Readings are intended as a guide to help you make changes to control your own life, not as a roadmap to blindly follow.

Methods of Divination

The tools we will discuss can be very helpful as something tangible to be able to either visually grasp the messages or clarify them. Because you are in human form, you may need to use your human senses such as sight or touch in order to translate universal messages or energy. I will go over a few popular methods of divination and you can decide if you want to use them or which one works best for you. Every Lightworker has a different extrasensory strength, and, depending what your psychic strength is, it will help you determine which method works best for you. If your powers of clairvoyance (clear seeing) are heightened, then perhaps you should go with a method that is very visual. If you feel your sense of touch (clear feeling) is heightened, perhaps the method for you is something tactile or that you can hold in your hand. Here are different psychic abilities you can chose from to determine which tool is best for you. Pick which sensation you feel you best respond to.

∞ Clairvoyance (seeing, or psychic vision).

∞ Clairaudience (hearing, or psychic hearing).

∞ Clairsentience (feeling/sensing, or psychic feeling/sensing).

∞ Claircognizance knowing, or psychic knowing).

∞ Clairgustance (tasting, or psychic tasting).

∞ Clairalience (smelling or psychic smelling).

Whichever method suits your personal inclination is the tool or tools you should work with. No divination tool is better than the other; it is simply a matter of what works best for you.

The Tarot

Thousands of years old, the true origin of these ancient cards is really unknown. A standard Tarot deck consists of 78 cards made up of the Major and Minor Arcana. The Major Arcana signifies the most important life issues and occurrences, while the Minor gives us more detail on the subject and is broken down into four suits: cups (love and emotions), wands (business and enterprise), swords (thoughts and intellect), and pentacles (money and finance). The cards are laid out in a certain way, the most common being the Celtic cross and answers to your question are translated by placement in the spread and card definition.

The cards, which document the entire soul's journey from birth to death, have standard definitions, but I have found that certain cards represent different things for different readers. Images on the cards seem to jump out at you if they hold a particular significance to your question. So with the Tarot, watch what jumps out and calls your attention on the card. The best practice is to learn the meaning of each card and then use these guidelines to help you understand their personal messages for you.

∞ What catches your eye on the card?

∞ What emotions do you feel?

∞ How do the details in the picture reinforce those ideas?

∞ What is the overall mood?

∞ What do you think this card might mean?

Astrology

Meaning science of the stars, astrology can give us insight into our lives by the position of the planets at the time of our birth. Astrology can give you a deeper understanding of all your relationships, career paths, and other aspects of your life by understanding your birth chart and examining the positions of the planets. This analysis points out areas to challenge and fulfill your individual destiny. There are 12 signs of the zodiac and when you were born indicates which astrological sign you fall under and your characteristics. Many people enjoy comparing astrological charts to determine romantic compatibility; here is a list of each sign and their dates.

∞ Aries: March 21-April 20

∞ Taurus: April 21-May 21

∞ Gemini: May 22-June 21

∞ Cancer: June 22-July 22

∞ Leo: July 23-August 21

∞ Virgo: August 22-September 23

∞ Libra: September 24-October 23

∞ Scorpio: October 24-November 22

∞ Sagittarius: November 23-December 22

∞ Capricorn: December 23-January 20

∞ Aquarius: January 21-February 19

∞ Pisces: February 20-March 20

By examining the position of the planets and planetary cycles and then comparing them to your natal chart (position of the planets at the time of your date of your birth, time and place), you can determine things such as:

∞ Personality traits.

∞ Outlooks for the future.

∞ Relationship potentials.

∞ Career path.

∞ Health issues.

∞ Financial matter.

∞ Life path.

The I Ching

A Chinese divination method, I Ching is one of the oldest and has traditionally been practiced throughout the Asian world. I Ching is a very powerful divination tool that brings solutions and answers to any number of life questions. The I Ching falls into a category of divination called geomancy, as it uses the numerical arrangements of patterns and objects (usually coins or stalks) thrown at random to define future happenings and gain insight into our lives.

Ouija board

Ouija is a mediumship tool. There are many warnings and fears associated with the Ouija board, but talking boards as methods of divination certainly have been used for centuries. These boards constitute a form of mediumship and communication with the spirit world. We can communicate with our guides this way to seek knowledge and guidance. First, we have to make sure our intentions are set and we use the board with integrity in order to attract the right entity on the board.

This method of divination can be uncertain, because although a spirit may want to help guide, they are not all-knowing and all-seeing. Also spirits have been known to mislead or create confusion either unintentionally or on purpose.

Numerology

Numerology is the study of the symbolism of numbers. This practice embraces the concept that each number carries a universal vibration and coincides with different personality traits, inner needs, and personal strengths. Each single digit from 1 to 9 is called a life path number. Numerology charts can get quite complex and detailed, but the simple formula to discovering your personal life path number goes this way:

Example Birth date: December 25, 1986 or 12/25/1986

- ∞ December (12) 1+2 = 3
- ∞ (25) 2+5 = 7
- ∞ (1986) 1+9+8+6 = (24) ... 2+4 = 6
- ∞ Now add the numbers together: 3+7+6 = (16) ... 1+6 = 7
- ∞ Your Life Path Number is 7

Numerology presents the whole picture, revealing all the diverse parts of your personality and how they come together to create the person you are. The following is an overview of each life path number and its meaning.

- ∞ Life Path 1: Independent. You are a born leader who would do best being your own boss. The negative aspect of the 1 energy is that you may become too self-serving or egotistical.

- ∞ Life Path 2: Partnerships. You see both sides easily and you make an excellent mediator. There is sincere concern for others. You think the best of people, and want the best for them. The negative aspect of the 2 energy is that you can become very pessimistic and experience difficulty in getting things done due to your passivity.

∞ Life Path 3: Creative. Many threes are writers, actors, or artists. Your optimistic nature often lifts others up. The negative aspect of the 3 energy is you may wish to escape when things start to become too heavy. Also it is not uncommon with the 3 life path to find it very hard to settle into a daily routine.

∞ Life Path 4: Organized. Practical, trustworthy, and down-to-earth, you are an excellent organizer and planner because of your innate ability to view things in a very common sense and practical way. The negative 4 tends to get too caught up in the daily routines and often you fail to see the big picture and major opportunities that could come along.

∞ Life Path 5: Adventurous. You can't seem to sit still. Your energy is magnetic and persuasive. You enjoy your freedom and are a good communicator, and you know how to motivate people, making you an excellent teacher. The negative of the 5 energy is you seek adventure to the extent of becoming self-indulgent and totally unaware of the feelings of those around you.

∞ Life Path 6: Compassionate. You have a warm, loving disposition. You are nurturing of others, and your favorite things are family and home. You have a strong sense of responsibility and are idealistic. The 6 must feel useful to be happy. The negative aspect of the 6 energy is a tendency to become overwhelmed by responsibilities and be a slave to others.

∞ Life Path 7: Thinker. You are a deeply spiritual, intuitive, reserved, and analytical person. Not a social person, your reserve is often taken as aloofness. The negative of the 7 energy is you tend to become very pessimistic, lackadaisical, quarrelsome, and secretive if you are not living a fulfilling life.

∞ Life Path 8: Visionary. You see the whole picture and you are often focused on security. You are usually very independent, forceful, and competitive. The negative aspect of the 8 energy is material achievements and rewards can become a priority for you, even to the neglect of family, home, and peace of mind.

∞ Life Path 9: Humanitarian. You like helping others and are a humanitarian. You have a compassionate spirit. Like Life Path 1, you are also a born leader. The purpose of life for those with a 9 life path is of a philosophical nature. The negative aspect of 9 energy is those under this vibration must be prepared to give up all personal desire and ambitions for your humanitarian role and push ego aside.

Beyond this cycle of nine, there are the Master Numbers 11, 22, and 33. These never are reduced to single digits.

∞ Life Path 11: Master Intuitive. You are highly sensitive and intuitive. Your life path is somewhat extreme, avant-garde, idealistic, visionary, and cultured. You should use your gifts to help others. You connect with others on a spiritual level. The negative aspect of the 11 energy is the tendency to harbor feelings of dissatisfaction with accomplishments and personal progress in life. You are related to Life Path 2.

∞ Life Path 22: Master Builder. This is the most powerful Master number. Your thoughts have the power to manifest in reality. You are spiritual and help others succeed. You are also a practical idealist who is concerned with the benefit and progress of humanity. The negative aspects of the 22 energy is to become very dictatorial, insensitive, and overbearing. You are related to Life Path 4.

∞ Life Path 33: Master Teacher. You are the rarest of the Master numbers and the Master Teacher. You will want to use your life to raise the consciousness of as many people as possible. You may become a spiritual leader and teacher. You have unending energy. Your core is that of a compassionate humanitarian. The negative of the 33 energy is becoming overwhelmed and having a tendency toward addictions. You are related to Life Path 6.

Pendulum

Using a pendulum is a fairly easy way to get simple yes or no answers. Your pendulum can be a crystal strung on a long chain, a special pendant you wear, or even your favorite necklace. The actual instrument doesn't really matter and is a personal preference. When you ask a particular question, your higher-self will find the answers and you will begin to subconsciously swing the pendulum in the direction of yes or no to give you the response.

The response action can be different for everyone, so you must first test your pendulum to see what direction it will swing in for different answers. These are some of the motions in which a pendulum responds.

- ∞ Clockwise or circular right.
- ∞ Counter-clockwise or circular left.
- ∞ Diagonally left.
- ∞ Side-to-side.
- ∞ Diagonally right.
- ∞ Back and forth.

Ask a simple question to which you know the answer to test how your pendulum responds. For example, if I asked, "Is my name Sahvanna?" the direction in which it swings would be the yes movement of the pendulum. If I asked, "Is my name is Susan?" the direction in which it swings would be a no response. Once you determine the response movements of your pendulum, you may begin to ask it questions to which you do not know the answer.

If the swing is modest at first, don't be concerned, because once you make the connection to the answer, the pendulum will swing wildly in one direction or another, and there will be no doubt as to what the answer is.

These are just a few of many tools of divination you can use. You can use one or several to help you gain guidance and wisdom. Remember, all the answers are there for you already, and these tools are an excellent companion to your already acute Lightworker gifts.

13
Support From Higher Realms

For many years, we have lived here on earth with the energetic scales unbalanced. Fear was controlling us and those on the higher planes needed to send help fast. By sending souls with increased light energy, slowly the scales began to tip back into balance, thus creating a new collective consciousness that is more aware and a new age of enlightenment is emerging. We are beginning to see that where once only science, logic, and rationality were our main frames of reference, now we are open to what we cannot see or what may have seemed illogical. By sending this wave of light to earth, our guides and teachers of the higher realms have assisted humanity in seeing more of the whole picture. We will never see it all from where we stand here on earth, but at least they give us a light in the darkness.

As a race, we are upon a time of great change in consciousness and awareness. This is a time when we are finally aware that we can unlock the powers of the spirit and still utilize them, even though we are in physical form.

As long as our consciousness is rooted in our physical bodies and physical awareness, we see things in only concrete forms, good or bad, positive or negative. This human mentality creates judgment and separation, but in the universe, there is no separation. There is only oneness. To achieve oneness, we need to place our consciousness beyond judgment and beyond separations. This is the shift that is happening now. Because of all the light energy being sent to earth, we cannot help but elevate our collective consciousness and create this type of shift from the "we" to the "I" state of awareness, bringing the new hope of peace and love for all mankind.

When the energy of the universe is balanced, it creates a lack of resources to create war, dissention, and discontent. Thus, a new wave of light was meant to save both our planet and mankind. Who oversees this wave of light that is now infiltrating our energy field? There are masters of wisdom who are never far away. Without our overseers, we would be lost in the darkness, but these beings of love and wisdom from the higher realms will not allow that to happen. They are the ascended masters and archangels who oversee the Lightworkers who are sent to earth. They have sent them here to heal the earth and will continue to send more as needed.

As a Lightworker, you are never alone in your task. These beings of love and wisdom of the higher realms are here for you, to support you and guide you in your work. All you need to do is call upon them and they will spring to action. No question is insignificant or too trivial. These beings of wisdom and love are the overseers of humanity and want to help. Archangels and Ascended Masters hold the vocation of your tutelage and are always waiting to be of service to you. Let's first look at some of the Ascended Masters first, who they are, and what they specialize in.

Who oversees the Lightworkers?

Ascended Masters belong to the sixth plane. This realm is reserved for those of only the highest frequency—just before Source. These spiritually enlightened beings were once mere mortals and now, near completion of their spiritual evolution, have limitless powers. They are our source personified, having ascended into the next level above human and are now part of all that is divine, pure, and powerful. At times they may come to earth in physical form to serve humanity. This can be when there is to be a major shift in consciousness or a time of great enlightenment. They may come with great notoriety or by some magnificent display of divine expression. Or, they may come in silence and create transformation for mankind unrevealed.

Ascended Masters serve as the overseers of humanity and utilize all gifts of the higher realms to serve us. They also come and go at will from the Earth plane without experiencing birth or death. Just as Jesus (an Ascended Master) was born to a virgin, there is no need for an ascended master to go through the process of being conceived, because they are perpetual beings of heavenly energy. Jesus Christ was the first to come forth to reveal his Ascended Master status. He showed it is possible to supersede the conception process, heal others, die, and rise again while still here on earth. They are not bound by time and space; lifetime after lifetime, they come and go at will. They have let go of all material lessons, balanced karma, and will take action as the universal creator in the physical form when needed.

But the Ascended Masters are not confined to earth. They work everywhere in the universe with complete freedom, transcending all human limitation; they are the embodiment of what we discuss in this book with their ability to separate spirit from the confines of the human-self. These glorious beings, who guard and help the evolving human race, are our greatest teachers, guardians, and advocates. They are the ones responsible for sending the waves of Lightworkers to heal humanity.

Some examples of Ascended Masters you may know are Jesus Christ, Buddha, and the Blessed Virgin Mary, but there are many more. These are just some and those who are choosing to work closest with the Earth at this time. There are an endless number of Ascended Masters working in other galaxies, universes, and even multi-universes.

The following is a list of the Ascended Masters in alphabetical order, and a brief description of their abilities and characteristics. You can call upon these beings in times of need, and they will guide you with their all-knowing, all-powerful universal love. To call upon them, simply say their names and then state your request. The invocation should go as follows: "[Name of Ascended Master], please help me to [state your request] at this time of need and for always."

If there happens to be a specific color associated with the Ascended Master, envision the color surrounding you as you invoke their assistance. If you feel a particular connection to a particular Master, or some more than others, this indicates that they are working with you in this current incarnation.

∞ Akshobhya: The immovable one is the embodiment of "mirror knowledge," a knowledge of what is real, and what is illusion, or a mere reflection of actual reality. Associated with the element of water, his color is blue and his attributes include the bell, three robes, a staff, a jewel, a lotus, a prayer wheel, and a sword. His lotus throne is supported by the elephant, which represents steadfastness and strength. He represents what is immovable. Call upon him to overcome passions, such as anger and hatred toward other beings.

∞ Amogasiddha: Almighty conqueror or Lord of Karma. His color is green. Call upon him to protect you from envy and jealousy.

∞ Amen Bey: He is here to help with the inner being and serve the youth of humanity. We have internal conflict, internal barriers, past-life bonds, and vows which limit us. Call upon him to remove unseen limitations, and to help young adults remove emotional blocks and achieve healing.

∞ Amerissis: She is a powerful being who is devoted to the light of God in every part of life. Call upon her when you wish to expand your light energy.

∞ Amethyst: She is also known as Holy Amethyst. She guards the powers of invocation. Her color is violet. Call upon Amethyst for assisting in developing tolerance and diplomacy.

∞ Anubis: The Egyptian god Anubis was associated with the mummification and protection of the dead for their journey into the afterlife. He is a walker between worlds and knows the path that goes from the physical to nonphysical. Call upon Anubis to guide those on journeys between worlds.

∞ Apollo: The Sun god who oversees prophecy, light, music, and healing. Call upon Apollo for happy endings to stressful situations, protector from evil, and assistance with psychic abilities.

∞ Ashtar: He is an Intergalactic Ascended Master, an extraterrestrial being that guides and protects mankind, helping to create a peaceful Universe. Ask his help with your acsension path and when praying for world peace.

∞ Babaji: Is an Unascended Master. He has chosen to stay on earth with a physical body, until all of humanity ascends. This is a service of great value as his presence anchors the Light of the higher planes into the earth. Ask for his help when you need to call on light energy or for grounding purposes.

∞ Buddha: His name means "awakened or enlightened one." Ask his assistance for forgiveness of yourself, protection against harmful thoughts, and sacrifice and giving of one's self.

∞ Cyclopea: Is known as the all-seeing eye of God. Call upon him for truth, healing, and knowledge.

∞ Dom Ignacio: He is best known as the Ascended Master working with the healer John of God in Brazil. Call upon him for healing purposes.

∞ El Morya: He comes to us to embody the qualites of obedience to holy will. His color is blue. Call upon him for will, faith, protection, and power.

∞ Hilarion: He works to help you gain mastery in the third-eye chakra. His color is emerald green. Call upon him when you need assistance with music, science, and focused "vision" through the perceptions of the third eye.

∞ Jesus Christ: He teaches us about love and forgiveness. Jesus was also known to be a great healer of sickness. Call upon Jesus for clear communication with God, divine guidance and direction, faith issues, forgiveness, healing of all kinds, manifestation, and miracles.

∞ John the Baptist: He became an Ascended Master in his life as Elijah, the prophet. He will help you with your ascension path through meditation. Call upon him to help align your divine mind, sacred heart, and soul.

∞ Kali: She will assist you in the transformation of energy. When you need to let go of the old and bring in the new, she frees you of fear, and she will abolish that which holds you back or slows or diverts your divine purpose. Call upon Kali for courage, determination, direction, focus, motivation, and tenacity.

∞ Kuan-Ti: The Chinese warrior god who acts to prevent war, he is a prophet who predicts the future and protects people from lower spirits. He works with Archangel Michael to help resolve matters of justice within government systems. Call upon him for justice and freedom for the falsely accused, prisoners of war, and legal matters.

∞ Kuan Yin: She is the goddess of mercy, compassion, and unconditional love. She is known as a great healer, and works to mainly heal the emotional body. She comes to help us with our internal battles and has a powerful maternal energy. Many call to her to help resolve fertility issues and help conceiving a child.

∞ Lakshmi: She is the Hindu goddess of wealth, prosperity (both material and spiritual), fortune, and the embodiment of beauty. Her colors are deep rose or gold. Call upon her for space-clearing and beautifying your home or surroundings.

∞ Lord Lanto: The Lord of Illumination. His color is a bright yellow. Lord Lanto teaches the path of enlightenment and mastery through the crown chakra. Call upon him for clarity of purpose, clarity of understanding, and illumination of the truth.

∞ Lu-Hsing: He works with salaries, pay success, progress, steady accumulation of wealth, and prosperity. Call upon him for matters of employment, seeking employment, job interviews, and raises and promotions.

∞ Lugh: He works to help humans develop their inner sorcerer or sorceress with divine love. He is associated with fertility and yielding a bountiful summer harvest. Call upon Lugh to assist in healing from painful situations, protection of all kinds, and solutions to any problem.

∞ Ma'at: She is the Egyptian goddess of truth, fairness, and justice. She is also the goddess of integrity and promises. Call upon her for balance, help with curing addictions, cravings, and purifying the body.

∞ Maitreya: He brings great compassion and is committed to bring happiness to earth. Maitreya means "Loving One." Call upon him when joy, laughter, and a sense of humor are needed.

∞ Mary Magdalene: Her twin flame is Jesus and we associate her most from time with Jesus 2000 years ago, but she has had many lives since then, just finally making her ascension in the last 20 years. Her colors are pink and magenta. Call upon her to help those who are in personal crisis or in need of finding their personal power.

∞ Merlin: A sage-wizard and powerful magician, he is a spiritual teacher and psychic visionary. Call upon Merlin when you need assistance with working with crystals, energy work, healing, and divination.

∞ Mother Mary: As the mother of Jesus, she was already an Ascended Master, having attained her ascension in a previous life. Call upon her for assistance in dealing with issues relating to children, support for those who help children, fertility, and healing of all kinds.

∞ Moses: A prophet who helped lead people out of slavery. Call upon Moses for assistance with authority figures, courage, leadership, and negotiating with others.

∞ Lady Nada: She will assist you in mastering peace, service, and brotherhood through the solar-plexus chakra. Her colors are purple and gold. Healing is part of her services to mankind. Call upon her when you need to heal your inner child.

∞ Paul, the Venetian: Lord of divine love, compassion, and charity. His color is pink. He teaches the way of love through wisdom. Ask his assistance when you need to heal or open your heart chakra or in all matters associated with beauty, patience, understanding, self-discipline, discernment, and unconditional love for yourself and others.

∞ Ratnasambhava: He is the source of all things precious. His color is yellow. He is associated with the element of earth. The embodiment of compassion, call upon him for protection against pride and unhealthy desire, and for grounding purposes as well.

∞ St. Germain: He releases all that binds and hinders the full expression of the soul into liberating light. His color is violet. Call upon St. Germain for forgiveness, freedom, alchemy, transmutation, justice, and mercy. Call upon him for help with legal issues and also to release you from any situation that hinders your progress.

∞ Sanam Kumara: A cosmic Master, he is so vast, he has to manifest a body for the Ascended Masters to see him. His color is gold. Call upon him for enlightenment and healing.

∞ Serapis Bey: He assists with harmony in working with others and discipline. His color is white. Call upon him for teamwork or serving in groups harmoniously and supporting one another in work or charitable situations.

∞ St. Francis: The advocate of animals and pets, call upon him for animal communicating and healing. He also works with troubled youths.

∞ St. Padre Pio: He was a priest from Italy who is venerated as a saint in the Catholic Church. Call upon him for help in ailments that deal with eyesight, including blindness, as well as forgiveness, and increasing the abilities of healing of all kinds. Vairochana: Call upon him to clear away ignorance and delusion. His color is white.

Ascended Masters exist to educate and help humanity expand its consciousness beyond human awareness. These are powerful, real beings who once and could now be walking the earth with us to serve as guardians and powerful protectors of mankind. Without them we would be lost, but there is no fear because they will never abandon humanity. These loving beings of light and wisdom are with us always and give protection and guidance to all persons, places, and things that are in need. Remember, they are always here for you and their guidance and protection is just a request away.

14
The Archangels

The Archangels are the highest rank in the celestial hierarchy and they are much larger and more powerful than other types of angels we know of, such as guardian angels or cherubs. The Archangels have specific jobs and duties and are ready and waiting to help anyone, anywhere, at any time who invokes their assistance. Because they are non-denominational, they are available to assist people of all cultures and belief systems. They are not bound by space or time, so they can be many places at once. The Archangels respect and follow the laws of free will and will never intervene without your request or permission, so it is necessary to ask for their help. You can also ask for their assistance on behalf of another person (that is, in the case of sickness, guidance, or any situation), but this person must be willing to accept their help. When you invoke the assistance of the Archangels, you are bringing in strong, powerful energies that can guide you in life purpose, healing, and many other aspects of your incarnation.

There are an endless number of Archangels who are working with Source to oversee the universe, but here is a list of some of those who are working closely with humanity, their duties, and how you can invoke their loving guidance.

Ariel

Archangel Ariel is aligned with the natural world and animals, and assists in conservation of our natural world. His name means "lion of God." Ariel will work alongside Archangel Raphael for healing both wild and domestic animals. If you find an injured bird or other wild animal that needs healing, call upon Ariel for help. When Ariel is working closely with you, you may notice many references to lions being brought into your awareness. Call upon Ariel for support in animal rescue causes or those who work in animal rescue.

Invocation for Archangel Ariel

I call forth the power and the presence of the Archangel Ariel. I desire to help heal the earth's environment, and I ask you to give me this divine intention in my life. I ask that you clear the path and support me in my mission. Thank you for the joy that my work will bring to me and the world.

Azrael

Azrael's name means "whom God helps." His primary role is to help people cross over to heaven at the time of physical death. He keeps track of lives by recording the births of the living and erasing the names of those who have died. He will bring comfort to those who are near their physical passing, making sure they don't suffer during death, and he helps them assimilate to life in the nonphysical. He will also surround grieving family members with healing energy and help them deal with the pain of loss. Call upon Azrael to assist you through the grieving process when the loss of a loved one occurs. Azrael also assists those working through important life lessons, helping to release guilt, anger, and regret, and eventually find forgiveness

Invocation for Archangel Azrael

Archangel Azrael, please comfort me now. Please help me to heal. Please help me to feel the connection to my beloved who has moved on. Please lift my heart and through cleansing tears let me see the blessings that this situation holds. Please watch over me, with healing light to carry me through my grief and pain. Thank you, Azrael.

Chamuel

The Archangel of pure love, Chamuel can lift you from the depths of sorrow and find love in your heart. His name means "he who seeks God." Chamuel will assist you in strengthing the bonds within relationships you have already formed, or helping you create new relationships with others you can connect with, or even your soulmate. The other areas you can invoke Chamuel for is in working with the heart chakra. If you feel your heart chakra has closed or is in need of cleansing, Chamuel will assist you in doing this. Healing grief and depression is also part of his work. Chamuel works in healing the heart after divorce or separation, strengthening the parent/child bond, and releasing negative feelings toward others. Chamuel is the patron angel of all who love God.

Invocation for Archangel Chamuel

I ask beloved Archangel Chamuel to assist me in becoming the divine expression of love and all that it embodies. Please help me to remove all negative thoughts that cloud my vision, and go forward with only love in my heart for all those who share the light. Thank you.

Gabriel

Gabriel is known as the "messenger" angel, and his name means "the Divine is my strength." Known as the angel that announced the coming birth of Christ, this Archangel also helps anyone whose life purpose involves art or communication. Gabriel is also the patron of all who work in the field of writers, journalists, clergy, and even postal workers. Call on Gabriel to assist you with any kind of communication, whether it is talking openly with a loved one or expressing yourself or emotions. If you are a writer and experience writers block, call upon Gabriel to release the messages you need to give to the world. Gabriel also aids in child conception or the process of adopting a child. If you are considering starting a family, call upon Gabriel.

Invocation for Archangel Gabriel

I invoke the mighty and powerful Archangel Gabriel to bring me assistance. Please bring me insights on how to speak my truth for the greatest good of all and release any negative energy associated with my words, now and always. Remove all my doubts and fears, and purify my body, mind, and spirit. I honor and thank you Archangel Gabriel for granting this, my wish.

Haniel

For harmony, good company in our lives, and loving relationships, call upon Haniel. This Archangel will also help you stay poised before and during any important event, such as a speech, presentation, first date, or job interview. Archangel Haniel oversees the powers of intuition. Call upon Haniel to help you with your psychic or extra-sensory perceptions.

Archangel Haniel, please bring your divine energy of loving wisdom to guide me in trusting my intuition. Help me communicate my words, actions, and mannerisms to bring peace and harmony to others and grant blessings to everyone who sees or hears me. Thank you, glorious Haniel.

Jeremiel

Jeremiel is the Archangel who reviews our lives with us after we've crossed over. His name means "mercy of God." He is also able to do this for us while we're still living, helping us to review or take inventory of our life so we can correct the wrongs we've done by making positive adjustments. Calling upom Jeremiel is very important because his actions allow us to make the changes needed to put us on the right path.

Invocation for Archangel Jeremiel

Archangel Jeremiel, please help me to see clearly the mistakes I have made. I humbly ask for the opportunity to correct what errors I have made without guilt or reservation. Allow me to love and forgive myself unconditionally. Please clearly give me guidance about anything that I may do or change to create the highest and best future for myself and all concerned. Thank you.

Jophiel

The Archangel of art and beauty, his name means "beauty of God." Jophiel will help artists or interior decorators with their artistic projects. Call upon Jophiel when you need to think beautiful thoughts and to see and appreciate beauty around you, including the beauty in others. Jophiel helps to cleanse and beautify the planet and can be called upon for help in environmental causes or concerns. Jophiel is also there to assist Lightworkers in their awakening process, allowing them to recognize their authentic selves and the divine intention of their lives.

Invocation for Jophiel

I now invoke the power and beauty of Archangel Jophiel. Please help me to see the magnificence and bliss that is within the entire universe. Please free me from depression and despair, and help me to know the beauty that is within myself as is within all creation. Thank you.

Metatron

One of the only two Archangels whose name does not end in "el" and one of the only two Archangels who were humans before becoming Angels (his brother Sandalphon being the other). The meaning of his name is unknown. Metatron is the youngest of the archangels. Because Metatron excelled at his work on earth, he was given the job to scribe the records of everything that happens on earth and keep the Akashic records, or the *Book of Life*. Call upon Metatron when you feel overwhelmed and he will make the stressful situation more manageable. Metatron will help you prioritize, organize, and focus on your goals and aspirations. He also works especially closely with children, particularly those who are spiritually gifted.

Invocation for Archangel Metatron

Archangel Metatron, I ask for your powerful and loving assistance in organizing and prioritizing my life. Please allow me the clarity to see what is most significant to my spiritual growth and what will allow me to pursue my divine intention set forth in my soul plan. Thank you, Metatron.

Michael

Michael is the leader of all the Archangels and is in charge of protection, courage, strength, truth, and integrity. His name means "who is like God" or "like unto God." Michael is a great and powerful protector and will make sure all who call upon him are safe from harm. He also oversees the Lightworker's life purpose. Michael carries a giant sword that he uses to cut through any negative attachments that hinder our progress and you can ask Michael to used his sword to cut any negative attachments to people, places, or situations. Michael is working with earth at the present time to rid us of the harsh energies associated with fear. Michael helps us to understand our true mission as a Lightworker, and will assist you in all areas of protection, space-clearing, and the release of fear-based energy.

Michael is also the patron of law enforcement and will assist in the protection of anyone who works in this field, because he helps with heroic deeds and bravery. You will be made aware of Michael's presence by seeing flashes or blue lights or purple sparkles in your peripheral vision.

Invocation for Archangel Michael

I now invoke the mighty and powerful Archangel Michael to come to my assistance. Please grant me the strength, courage, and honor I need to fulfill my life purpose. Please use your sword to cut away any doubts or negativity. Surround me with your protection, and grant me the courage and bravery to overcome and release my fears. Thank you.

Raguel

He is often called the Archangel of Justice and Fairness, and his name means "friend of God." Call upon Raguel whenever you feel you're being overpowered because he is the defender of the underdogs. You can also call upon Raguel on behalf of another person who is being unfairly treated. Call on him when you need to be empowered and respected. He helps to resolve arguments, helps with cooperation, and leads to harmony in groups and families. Raguel also oversees the other Archangels to ensure all are working harmoniously and productively with humanity.

Invocation to Archangel Raguel

I ask the invocation of the powerful and mighty Archangel Raguel to assist me in my plight. Please help me to find my strength and personal power in this situation and all others in the future. Help me to work harmoniously with the greatest good for all involved. Help me to overcome any negativity and unfairness that I encounter along the way. For this, I humbly thank you.

Raphael

The Hebrew word *rapha* means "doctor" or "healer" and Raphael means "healing power of God." He is a powerful healer and assists with all forms of healing, both physical and spiritual. Raphael assists doctors, therapists, and surgeons in their work and will also assist those who are learning to be healers or entering into the healing profession. Other areas Raphael helps with is finding lost pets, and reducing and eliminating addictions and cravings.

Raphael is known as the patron of travelers. Call upon Raphael when you are traveling, to assure safe travel. Raphael also helps with inward spiritual journeys, and assisting in searches for truth and guidance. You will be made aware of Raphael's presence when you see sparkles or flashes of green light. Part of Raphael's healing work involves spirit rescue and the clearing of earthbound spirits. He often works with Michael to exorcise discarnate entities as well.

Invocation for Archangel Raphael

I now invoke the mighty and powerful Archangel Raphael to stand before me. Please fill me with light energy and good health. Help me heal the wounds from the past. Please heal and restore every aspect of my being, body, mind, and soul. Thank you.

Raziel

Raziel works very closely with the Creator and its believed he knows all of the secrets of the Universe and how it operates. His name means "secrets of God." He wrote down all of these secrets in *The Book of the Angel Raziel*. Raziel can help you understand esoteric material, manifestation principles, and also increase your five senses and open you up to higher levels of psychic abilities. Raziel can also assist you with manifestations and receiving divine guidance.

Invocation for Archangel Raziel

Archangel Raziel, please help me open my awareness to the divine secrets of the Universe. Help me to release any restrictive views or fears so that I may receive divine guidance with depth and clarity. Thank you, Raziel, for teaching me.

Sandalphon

His name means "brother" in Greek, a reference to his twin brother, the archangel Metatron. The twins are the only archangels in heaven who were originally mortal men. Sandalphon's chief role is to carry human prayers to God, so they may be answered. He's said to be so tall that he extends from earth to heaven. Because Sandalphon knows from personal experience what it is to live as a mortal, he can assist you in your ascension process and is a wonderful assistant to those who are dedicated to a path of self-discovery, personal growth, and ascension. Sandalphon can help expectant parents determine the gender of their forthcoming child, and many also believe Sandalphon is also strongly associated with celestial music and serves as an angelic inspiration to musicians.

Invocation for Archangel Sandalphon

Beloved Archangel Sandalphon, deliverer and answerer of all prayers, I ask for your assistance now. I trust you to relay my message with clarity and urgency to a higher power. Please deliver my prayer to our Source Creator as soon as you can and serve as a divine messenger for my plea. Thank you, Sandalphon.

Uriel

Uriel is considered one of the wisest Archangels because of his intellectual information, practical solutions, and creative insight. His name means "God is light." He will shed light on all darkness and illuminate what is true. Uriel brings peace and harmony in the form of answers. He also brought the practice of alchemy to us and the ability to manifest from thin air, as well as give prophetic information and warnings. Uriel is also considered to be the Archangel who helps with earthquakes, floods, fires, hurricanes, tornadoes, natural disasters, and earth changes. Call upon Uriel to avert such events, or to heal those who need to recover in their aftermath.

Invocation of Archangel Uriel

I now invoke the mighty and powerful Archangel Uriel. Please help me to see what is true and authentic, and release any fears associated with my divine truth. Grant me tranquility and peace of mind. Help me to serve others and always walk in the light. Thank you.

Zadkiel

The Archangel of mercy and benevolence, Zadkiel can help you feel mercy and compassion toward yourself and others, and let go of judgment and practice forgiveness. His name means "the righteousness of God." Call upon Zadkiel to assist you in seeing the divine light within yourself and others, instead of focusing on the human identity and placing judgment. If you cannot find forgiveness for yourself or someone else, ask Zadkiel to intervene. Remember, forgiveness does not mean you are overlooking someone's abusive behavior, but it means you are freeing yourself of any energetic holds (guilt, fear, or negative attachments) they have placed on you.

Invocation of Archangel Zadkiel

Archangel Zadkiel, please help me find forgiveness and mercy to those who have harmed me. Help me find clarity and compassion in every situation I encounter. Calm my fears with faith and healing light to help me to now surrender this situation fully to you and to the universe. Thank you.

Remember, no request is too trivial or insignificant for the Archangels and they are here to help us live fuller and more compassionate lives. As you see, there is most likely an Archangel to call upon for every aspect of your life. They are never far away and always waiting for you to call upon them.

Part V

The Power of Self

15
Connecting With Telepathy

We have discussed different ways to explore outside human limitations, such as transferring energy and astral traveling in dreamtime. But is it possible to actually send messages through the power of telepathy to someone else? We have all seen the parlor tricks when a magician guesses what card a person is holding by "reading his mind," but what we will discuss is more profound than just a parlor trick. Telepathy or connecting with the consciousness of someone else should be done with the intent and purpose of healing or expanding the light energy of everyone involved. So, let's look at how you can develop your telepathic ability for not only practical use in everyday life, but for healing purposes as well.

My friend Justine and I took a class studying telepathy. One night, she decided to put what we learned to the test. She knew her husband William would be leaving work at 11 p.m. and every night on his route home, he passed a 24-hour diner. She decided to telepathically send William the specific message that she wanted a cheeseburger with lettuce, tomatoes, and a pickle. The house was quiet and she took the chance to lie on the couch and focus on her husband, sending him this message telepathically. She fixed the message in her mind, visualized the cheeseburger, and "sent" it to her husband. Eventually, she dozed off. She awoke when William entered the front door. Holding a white paper bag, he said, "Here Honey, I thought you would like a cheeseburger tonight!" Justine was amazed! She couldn't believe that William had received her message so clearly! William had no idea Justine had sent him the message with her mind, he just felt the urge to do something nice for his wife.

"Thank you!" she exclaimed, but as she opened her cheeseburger, she was disappointed to find no pickle. "You forgot the pickle," she told William.

"Damn! I told the waitress to put a pickle on it. She must have forgotten!" he answered. This clearly demonstrated that the mental connection between Justine and William was there and it was so powerful, Justine didn't have to call William on the phone, she could send him her dinner order directly through the cosmos!

Mental telepathy is not as uncommon as you may think; in fact many of us have telepathic experiences nearly every day, without even realizing it. Have you ever said, "Hey I was just thinking that!" when someone was speaking? Or have you ever known what someone would say before they say it? Couples who are energetically aligned often brag about "finishing each other sentences." This is no coincidence; there is a real transfer of consciousness occurring here and these types of experiences are actually telepathic in nature.

For most of us, telepathy will occur easily with someone who is close to us emotionally, such as a parent, spouse, or close friend. It never fails that when I call my mother she says "I was just going to call you!" This happens because the energetic bond is so powerful that it is easy to receive the thoughts of someone to whom you are so closely connected. You can also observe forms of telepathy in animals that are closely connected, such as schools of fish all acting in unison. What makes them all turn and swim in the same direction? There must be a collective consciousness that the close knit group shares and they can easily become like one mind. It is the same for humans. Because we all share space, this universal energetic chain, (just like the fish share space within the school), it is possible to tap into someone else's "wave" in the universal energy and pick up their thoughts or send them yours. It happens spontaneously all the time, but how do we consciously tap in so we can use this powerful ability to help, heal, and increase the light energy of the collective?

Different Types of Telepathy

Telepathy is not just mental (the exchange of thoughts). It can be physical and emotional as well. Let's look at how it can occur in our everyday lives in different ways, but we don't even realize it.

Physical telepathy

Have you ever heard stories about twins who claim to feel the same pain being experienced by their sibling, even when they are apart? In the animal world, how do geese know what direction to fly in or when they need to change formation? They certainly are not calling out to each other verbally in the sky. These examples are forms of physical telepathy. The physical body is responding and acting in sync with the collective consciousness of others around them as they seek to become like one. Because we learned that we do not have to be confined to the boundaries of the physical world, telepathy is easily practiced with those outside our immediate vicinity or with someone who is further down the energetic chain. Mental telepathy is less subject to distance from the person sending the messages, but even physical telepathy can overcome great distances. Because we all share the energetic connection, distance doesn't have to factor in and we can send healing to anyone anywhere.

Emotional telepathy

This occurs when you pick up the emotions of someone else. Not to be confused with empathy, (when you would actually take on the emotions as your own). Another form of emotional telepathy can occur when groups or large masses feel the same emotions. It's sometimes called "mob mentality" or "mass hysteria." Emotional telepathy is the transference of feelings (or emotions) from one person to another instead of specific thoughts or messages. This can happen when you are interacting with someone who is depressed, and suddenly you are aware that something is not right. You just know something is wrong. Would it be possible to all feel the emotions of love and compassion and pass it on to the collective human family?

Telepathy can be used in your Lightworker role to help and heal. It doesn't have to be just "mind reading," it is sending physical, emotional, and mental messages that can positively affect the actions, feelings, and well-being of others.

So as you see, we are affected by telepathy in many ways during the course of our everyday lives. If we harness with ability and use it with good intentions, we can reach others in a positive way and enhance their lives through the use of this practice. I suggest you begin slowly and just attempt to send some loving and positive thoughts to a loved one. The lighter the wave is, the easier it is to send.

Once you become adept in telepathy, you can begin to transmit more profound waves, such as physical healing or waves that foster emotional well-being in others.

Here is a technique to practice telepathy for the purposes of healing and expanding light energy:

1. Sender and Receiver: You are going to be the sender. Pick a receiver and discuss this with that person ahead of time. It is important to ask permission so you do not impose your wishes upon someone who is not in agreement. Once you have both agreed and concluded that you are open to this transmission occurring, decide in what form it is being sent: mental, emotional, or physical (for healing purposes).

2. Relaxation: Keep your surroundings calm and quiet. Get into a comfortable position. It is important to be as relaxed as possible, so use the conscious breath and quiet mind techniques. Of course, you may use any relaxation method you find best. Just be sure to clear your mind of unwanted thoughts. Because you are the sender, your focus will be to send your intended waves to the receiver.

3. Begin to Visualize: Close your eyes and begin to bring a clear picture of your receiver into focus. Imagining that he or she is just feet away from you. Focus on details, such as hair color, eye color, and skin tone. Begin to use your extra sensory perceptions to tune

in on even more details, such as textures and smells. You need to zone in on the true essence of your receiver.

4. Imagine a silver cord connecting the two of you. This tube is the channel through which your waves would be communicated to the receiver. If the wave is mental, picture the tube connecting your third eye (center of the forehead) to his or her third eye. If the wave is emotional, picture the tube connecting your heart chakra (center of the chest) to his or her heart chakra. If the wave is physical, picture the tube connecting your root chakra (base of the spine) to his or her root chakra.

5. Once the tube is in place, begin to channel the wave through the tube.

6. Transmission: As you transmit your wave through the tube, envision your intention and push this mental picture through the tube. Make the picture as vivid as possible. If the wave contains optimal health, envision what that looks like to you and push it through. If your wave contains a thought or specific message, push that through the tube with all your mental energy. Feel the pressure as it forces its way through the tube, and continue to push with all your will. Continue to stay relaxed and focused.

7. Feel the breakthrough: As you push, you will feel a certain "pop" or breakthrough that ensures the wave

has been transmitted. This popping sensation cannot be mistaken, because it brings a certain feeling of relief. This feeling of breaking through assures you that the wave has been transmitted. You may even fall asleep after the pop. If you do not feel this breakthrough after 15 minutes, then you must stop because it indicates the resistance is too strong from the receiver.

Protecting Yourself

Many of us are unwitting victims of emotional, physical, or mental telepathy that we do not wish for, living or working in close proximity of others who are sending out "waves" of telepathic energy that we pick up and inherit if we don't protect ourselves. Due to the heightened sensitivity of Lightworkers, you could find yourself highly susceptible to these waves. Affirming each day that "I reject that which is not my own and is not for my greatest good" will help keep the unhealthy waves of others from penetrating your energy. Stay away from crowds where extreme emotions, addictions (such as bars where alcohol is served), or protests which are not peaceful are happening. A group of people influenced by projections of negative waves of emotion can result in mass hysteria. Being a sensitive Lightworker, this is going to affect you more than someone who is less sensitive.

As you become more proficient in telepathy, you will be able to use it anytime you like. This is a powerful ability and one that has tremendous healing potential. We have come to a new level of consciousness that tells us that telepathy is real and it is something to be used with the highest of intentions. As a Lightworker, your role is to heal and share your light energy. Telepathy is a perfect practice for transmitting waves of love and compassion to help heal and expand your light energy and that of others around you.

16
Transferring Energy

Like one link in an endless chain, we all band together to create the combined force of everything there is. This energetic strand spans throughout the entire universe and out into eternity, much more than our own human sense of self can comprehend, but it is what connects us to everything else contained within the infinity of the universe. Within that thread, we all have our own eternal, energetic space or what some people refer to as our energy field or aura. Each aura is as distinct as the individual who keeps it, with different hues, temperatures, and intensities. This personal energetic field is with us everywhere we go in the universe. The dimension or plane we inhabit makes no difference in the physical or nonphysical; it is our true essence and will leave the physical body when the body can no longer hold it due to age or sickness. We have learned that our true essence is energetic and that the physical is really just dense matter that holds our spirit. Because we are all comprised of healing energy and this energy has no boundaries or limitations, the question can be asked, "Can we extend our energy out to others in order to help and heal?" The answer is yes. This is our remote healing ability. The electromagnetic force of source energy is the common strand that holds us all together to create the collective energy of our universe.

My client Patty and her sister Joyce were inseparable throughout their lives—not just sisters in the physical, but truly soul sisters. Only a few years apart in age, they shared all their major milestones together. They even had their first babies just two days apart and spent long nights in the maternity ward playing cards and chatting while they recuperated together. Throughout the years, as they raised their families, they spent every Christmas Eve together with their children at Joyce's home. After a night of food, dancing, and games, they would wait until midnight to open the presents. Tired and exhausted by the fun and excitement of the holiday evening, Patty and her family would stay overnight and they would all have breakfast together on Christmas morning. It had become a tradition.

One Christmas morning, after breakfast, the sisters sat in the living room and chatted as Joyce was putting gifts back into boxes and sorting what was under the tree from the night before. Joyce told Patty; "You know, I had the strangest dream last night." She looked a bit unsettled as she recounted it to Patty. "You and I were in a big field and just above a grassy knoll, I saw Dad appear." Their father Michael had died years earlier in a work-related accident. "He was illuminated by a silvery light." She explained. "And as we walked toward him, holding hands, he seemed to glow brighter and brighter with a beautiful shimmer. He told me to take his hand and said to 'step over.'" Joyce explained that in her dream she was frightened and told her father, "No, I do not want to, I want to stay here on this side of the knoll with Patty." He continued to urge her to take his hand and step over and told her not to be afraid, it was easy to just take his hand. In her dream, she held on to Patty's hand tightly and said she said she woke up with the strangest feeling.

Trying to reassure her sister, Patty tried to laugh it off and said she would be sure not to ride in any cars with Joyce or take any chances when they were together. About six months later, Joyce suddenly fell ill. She was just 47 and going back to college to pursue her dream of becoming a lawyer. Her family noticed she was weak and disoriented and soon tests showed that she had brain cancer. During Joyce's last days, Patty never left her side and while on her death bed, she held her hand. One day Patty read aloud to Joyce a passage from an Edgar Casey book on dying. As Patty read and held her sister's hand, she began to feel a steady rhythm from Joyce's hand, almost like this sway-ing sensation that moved upward. This force's sensation pushed and pulled steadily, as if it was ascending Joyce's body to break free. Patty was a student of metaphysics and knew she was feeling her sister's soul trying to work its way out of the body. Suddenly, after about an hour, the strange swaying sensation stopped, and at that moment, Joyce's heart monitor went flat. She was gone and Patty was assured, that just as her sister had dreamed, she was holding one hand and their father had her other hand to help her step over.

This story illustrates how Patty could actually feel the energy's pressure coming from her sister's hand. It was a tangible feeling, one so powerful that it was actually felt on a physical level. Now does this only happen when we die, or can we consciously push our energy out? Can this be done to connect with someone else (within the collec-tive energy chain) or share our own energy to help heal them?

Lightworkers harbor an increased amount of light en-ergy and have special healing qualities that they have mas-tered on the higher planes. Many Lightworkers are called to healing practices such as Reiki or other hands-on heal-ing therapies. But we do not actually need to touch the person we are transferring light energy to; we can transfer energy from a distance. Many healers and Lightworkers practice what they call remote healing or energy transfer to help people who are not near or cannot be touched. Because this healing energy is not physical, we do not need to use our hands at all. We can send the energy out with our intent alone.

There are many different methods to energy transfer. Here is a simple one you can practice yourself.

Energy Transfer Method

1. Before attempting to transfer energy, it is necessary to first quiet the mind and raise your own vibration. Transferring energy that is not properly grounded or of a high enough frequency will not be effective.

2. State your intention and make a clear request of the universe as to where this energy is going and what you wish to accomplish. If you wish to make an energetic connection with a particular person, request that it be so. I ask to be connected with [state name of person]. I ask that my energy be transferred for the highest good of [name] and all those involved. I send my energy to [name] to be utilized in the most healing and loving way possible.

3. Using either fingertips or palms, locate the chakra to which you wish to send energy. For example, if someone is having stomach issues, place your hands on your solar plexus. As your hand is stationary in its position, focus on the positive energy flow coming from it and also recall your request from step 2. You intuitively feel when the connection is made and now the intention is so.

4. At this point, you will continue to focus on the feeling of energy happening between your hands and the selected chakra. You must remain in a quiet mind mode because the more quiet the conscious mind (or ego) becomes, the higher the spiritual vibration will rise. The higher the energetic frequency you can achieve and sustain, the more healing and love-filled the energy will become. As you raise your frequency, you are now in a meditative state and become linked with the person in need of healing.

5. In your meditation, visualize the body/face of your subject and simultaneously focus on the feeling of energy exchange happening between your hands and the chakra to which you are sending the energy. You will begin to feel a connection being established with that person. You may feel a kind of pulling or tugging sensation from your chakra as healing energy is being transferred from you to your subject.

6. Breath into this connection and keep it going. Concentrate on the energy you are feeling through your hands and keep your breath at a steady pace. As you go deeper into this meditative state, you may begin to feel the urge to reposition your hands, which is fine. It indicates that you are being guided on a higher level to circulate more energy to different areas in need.

7. You will begin to feel the pulling sensation begin to subside. This is an indication that the time has come

to stop the remote session and the healing energy has been transferred. You can now affirm that the connection was made and it is time to disconnect from the person. Think of this as hanging up a telephone; you must disconnect or you might remain linked, which is not desirable. You can do this by making a brief statement: I am now disconnected from [name] and it is my intention that this energy was transferred for his/her best intent and purpose.

Once you have connected and achieved your goal of transferring energy, you will most likely fall asleep. When we are in that elevated place of transference, we enter into astral zone or perhaps an even higher dimension, and to do that, our physical bodies will usually go to sleep. At times, you may even go in to a sleep paralysis state where you are conscious, but you are unable to move your body. You may hear a loud vibratory sound, similar to a piano tuning fork. This is your ethereal body establishing a connection to another dimension. This is nothing to be afraid of—you do it all the time unknowingly when you are dreaming in other states of altered consciousness.

Remote healing is usually done in cooperation with the person receiving the healing. But this is not necessary because you can send remote healing energy to people (or even certain situations) you don't know who are suffering.

For example, earthquake victims or those who are experiencing some traumatic event somewhere in the world can benefit from your healing energy.

17

Incarnation, Ascension, and the Power of Oneness

As Lightworkers discover their authentic selves and unique purpose, the ultimate question becomes *What do I do now? How do I incorporate all this into my life?* They want to know how to begin to blend this new awareness of who they really are into their day-to-day existence and how to process it with the true intent and purpose they came here to carry out. There is no one path to living your unique purpose; it is a profoundly individual process that must unfold in its own time. We all have different soul plans and paths that we have structured for ourselves, so this makes ascension a very distinctive process. We have many lessons to learn in each incarnation, and we must master what we came here for in order to move up to the next level.

Lightworkers' healing mission will not be complete until they themselves have completed their own lessons and souls' plan for this lifetime. By doing this, you will expand your light energy and move up the realms until you achieve oneness with God, and Lightworkers who do not stay on the path to ascension will feel empty and un-fulfilled. This why it is important to find your own path and stay on it. We have discussed many ways of shifting your focus from the physical world to what is authentic and eternal, but we still remain in human form and must battle to allow our spiritual-self to take the lead while living in a physical world. Once we become aware, we must really shift our perspective on reality and life in general. All our lives we are told we must achieve material success. People with lots of money and things are always perceived as lucky or as better than the have not's. But are they really? Focusing on what we possess in the material world is not what ascension is all about. Because, as we have learned, the material is short-lived and it is only what we cannot see or touch that is eternal.

So in order to rise up, we must shift our focus out of what is tangible to what is intangible and real. Your life doesn't need to change drastically, so don't feel as if you need to give away all your belongings and open an or-phanage in a third-world country. That is not what this is all about. Remembering to balance and integrating all parts of yourself is important. Imagine your Source Creator, with unconditional love for everything contained within the universe. Even what we perceive as wrong or bad is embraced and loved without conditions. This is how we must strive to be as well.

There are those who travel into our life path and play a negative role, but there is a much bigger picture and these individuals have their own soul plan to fulfill and we certainly cannot fault them for that. The idea of pain instills fear in us and our ego seeks to avoid that at all costs. Fear is the biggest obstacle to ascension there is. As we discussed, the human side of you, the Id and Ego, will control your life with fear, which is the root of all negative emotion. Fear is necessary at times here on earth, for protection and preservation, but the Lightworker on the ascension path must balance the human need for fear and the spiritual need to release it—a precarious balance. Emotions such as anger, shame, and hatred all stem from fear, and fear belongs your mortality alone. The spirit or higher-self knows no fear.

Also, the human concept of what is good and what is bad must fade away. The higher-self's comprehension is way beyond the scope of any human judgment of what is good or what is bad. Within each fear-based emotion, there is the human judgment of the dark energy it creates. As we learn to accept, value, and recognize our own dark energy in a balanced manner, we integrate our own dark side and synergize all elements of ourselves, because if we are on the path to oneness, then there is no such thing as separation. Staying on the ascension path is to embrace every type of energy we possess, and every emotion, thought, or intention we have and integrate them into our authentic selves. As we ascend, we will naturally clear all the fear-based beliefs, and transmute all fear-based emotions into loving compassionate ones. It is just the natural process of eliminating the obstacles that being human present us with. Having compassion for all fragments of yourself will transmute any negative emotions and bring expansion of your light energy—that is what is truly healing.

12-Step Ascension Plan

As stated, ascension is a unique path that only you can discover and walk. Here are some helpful ways that will help you discover the path and stay on it.

1. *Know your higher-self: Know yourself as more than just flesh and bone. You have an essence that is your authentic self. Recognize its voice and trust it at all times. Doubting the voice of your higher-self will remove you from your path and take you off course.*

2. *Be unconditional love: Be your own source of unconditional love. Love is the healing force of the universe, and when you emanate this, only more good things can flow into your life.*

3. *Make gratitude a way of life: Gratitude cannot be just an emotion you have, but must be fully integrated*

into your life. For every pain, there is spiritual progress, for every loss, there will be something gained. Know that gratitude will fill any void you have and make you whole once again.

4. Understand that there is a divine plan: There is no randomness within the universe. You are too precious for random happenings to control you. We all plan our own ascension strategies and the higher-self always knows the plan. Know that although your human awareness may not understand, your higher-self is always there, gently guiding you to where you should be. Everything that occurs is all in the plan and is meant to happen.

5. Your thoughts create your reality: Just as in the spirit world, your thoughts, intentions, and emotions support your reality. You are the creator of your universe, and you can create a world of beauty and magnificence.

6. Release fear: Fear lowers your frequency and will weigh you down. Fear is only known to your mortal self. The higher-self is evolved beyond the comprehension of fear. It simply does not exist.

7. Practice forgiveness: Do not harbor anger or bitterness for others. Everyone has their own plan and at times painful lessons come from those we love and trust most. There is no retribution in God's eyes, only forgiveness.

8. Believe in your own power: Know that you possess all the power of your Source Creator. You are a powerful being without limitations. The only boundaries you have are the ones you place upon yourself.

9. Acceptance: Know that you are in the right place now and always will be. Accept what outcomes occur and do not attempt to change what is to be. Trust that all that occurs is for your greatest good.

10. Right your wrongs: You are in human form and humans are imperfect. Mistakes happen and if you make one, do your best to correct it, heal, and move on. You will reap as you have sown.

11. Know that you are eternal: Understand that everything you do in your lifetime will remain with you forever. No experience, lesson, or interaction is ever lost, but belongs to you forever. Be selective in what you want to bring into eternity with you. Eventually you will have to account for it through Karma, lessons, and so on.

12. Understand that separation does not exist: We are all one within the collective. Understand that the line you draw between you and your neighbor is an illusion. We are one—what you do to others; you do to yourself, and most importantly, to Source.

Ascension and Oneness

When we talk about ascension, we are referring to our journey to oneness. As we travel through the realms, we go higher and higher until our frequency becomes one with the Universe. That sounds wonderful, but to our human ego, it sounds a bit scary. If we become one with God or a part of all there is, do we cease to exist? What happens to your individuality when we finally attain this state of oneness that we are all supposed to want so badly? The answer is yes, you will always maintain your individuality and your sense of "self" will remain intact. You will always be you, although oneness is very different from what you are experiencing now.

Currently, time, space, and the limitations of your human-self play a large part in your existence; you are limited strictly by the nature of the place you live in. This is not the case when you ascend and achieve oneness. You are not restrained by anything, and the whole universe is yours to explore. Your higher-self will be the only identity that exists now and the human primal Id and fear-based Ego are no more. You are now comprised of only energy—no more heavy, dense matter (your body) to weigh you down. No more physical pain or suffering. You are as light as a feather, and fear and worry are not in your frame of reference anymore.

Although you are now one with all there is, you are still an individual, uniquely you, yet one with all there is because the concept of separateness does not exist, either. You are not alone—there are others around you who have also achieved this state of oneness and you will interact with them in loving relationships. You can visit and have companions just like you do now. You feel love just like you do now, only it is a type of love that surpasses the mortal comprehension of what love is and feels unlike any connection you have ever felt before. You will remember the lessons you have learned, and appreciate all the work you have done to get to the heavenly place where you have now arrived. You can reunite with loved ones (animals included) who have crossed over into the spirit world, no matter where they are. You can choose to stay near them for always, or maybe just visit.

The concept of time will be no more and you can travel through different periods to experience things you always wanted to, such as living in the Renaissance Period or perhaps witnessing the birth of Christ. You will know the entire mosaic of your lifetimes, which you have lived across time. If your favorite lifetime was as a male in 1932, you can live as that, or change anytime you like. You will be fully aware and conscious of all that.

You will be able to manifest thoughts into objects. No longer will you be constrained by the material and having to construct or build what you want. Your thoughts will manifest instantly and without limitations. You can construct your home with just your thoughts that are as real as the home you live in now. You can choose your favorite incarnational self to represent your energy. If you wish, you can create art and music more beautifully than you can ever imagine because it's made up of only your intentions and thought processes. There will be no need for instruments or materials, just pure intention. You can still have all the things you love and hold dear, and you will create them with a single thought—you will live as the creator of all you wish for.

Lightworkers have sacrificed and given of themselves to heal the planet and humanity as part of their ascension strategy. Many Lightworkers suffer on their path, but this suffering does not go unrecognized. Someday you will ascend to this glorious place of love and light and reap the rewards of your hard work. While here on earth, remember that you are the torch bearer, you are the beacon that shines so bright, you are the one who emanates love and compassion for all humanity. Keep your intentions high, your thoughts pure, and never allow your light to be dimmed, because the world needs you. Lightworkers, your time to shine is now.

Epilogue

Lightworkers are souls who carry the strong an inner urging to heal, enlighten, and expand the light energy of the planet. This inner urging is brought with them from the place they came from, and often leads them to helping professions such as teaching, nursing, or counseling. Those who have embarked upon a service profession or found an outlet for their inner stirrings are the lucky ones. There are many Lightworkers who have difficulty identifying just what this inner urging is and mistake it for an inability to find happiness or fulfillment in their lives. This confusion usually brings the Lightworker to a place of human weakness, as comfort must be found somewhere, and if spiritual comfort is not taking place, physical comfort is readily available in food, drugs, sex, or other unhealthy behaviors. This creates an inner conflict within the Lightworker that becomes a battle of identity.

It is imperative for Lightworkers to find their unique path and allow their authentic selves to take the lead in their lives. This means integrating certain practices into your life, and harmonizing body, mind, and soul with things such as meditation, mindful exercise, and energetic cleansing. It certainly never promised to be an easy ride when you decided to incarnate here to help lend a hand. At times, it may have felt like you were reading about an alien species from another planet, but the term Lightworker does not separate you from the rest or make you a part of a superior group. It is simply a type of soul. We are all on the journey to being one with our Source. Getting there is simply a matter of working hard to make a conscious effort to love unconditionally and align with the light energy of the planet. This choice gives everyone the ability to get on the Lightworker path.

The label Lightworker may create some misunderstanding because it seems as though it separates us from the rest of humanity, but we are all part of a collective family. As we discussed, all things are loved equally by God, so there is no implication of supremacy to the label, either. If we think of how cars travel down a highway, there may be a car three lengths ahead of you, but this does not mean this car is superior, it is just farther along down the road. Lightworkers are souls who have worked hard to develop their frequency and light energy, and although farther down the road, we are all on the *same* road. A Lightworker may just be closer to the destination.

Humanity always waits for a great leader to come and lead them to enlightenment, but there are many leaders, millions, in fact, waiting to come forward and share their knowledge and spiritual awareness with humanity. Because of their inner calling to serve, Lightworkers often feel different or isolated from others and can't quite put their finger on why they feel so detached. I have found that Lightworkers who are unaware of their path are nearly always solitary individuals, and actually feel more comfortable when alone. This is why the practices in this book are so important to you and the fulfillment of your divine intention—the work you came here to do. They will allow you to know and recognize your true self with no fear, and move forward without reservation.

Putting up with human traits comes with the territory of being here on earth to help. At times, I have seen Lightworkers absolutely exasperated with their humanness. It is ironic how the unaware Lightworker must battle the nature of the inner Lightworker, and the aware Lightworker must battle with the nature of the outer human! Only by going through all stages of human development and illusion will you be able to reveal your true identity. Just as a caterpillar must go through a metamorphosis to become a butterfly, you too must go through the stages of transformation.

Many of my clients come with questions of life purpose. People need to know they have a purpose, a reason for being, and they seek out the answer to that. I always counsel my clients to stop asking that question. The simple answer is that you are living your life purpose right now, today, as we speak. There is no need to question it or ask because it is happening on a daily basis, and it changes all the time! Our Source Creator did not put you in the human experience and say, "Okay, your mission is to find the cure for cancer!" Your mission is one that unfolds as you proceed along your path and expand your light energy. As we travel along our path, we fulfill many missions and purposes, and as we go forward, our purpose can shift and change, depending on the roads we choose.

There is no need to feel you're not where you are supposed to be or doing what you should be doing, because each experience, each interaction is forever in the memory of your soul and creates the energy that makes you. The information and practices within this book will guide you to mastery of your role, but mastery is different for all of us; mastery is specific to your own ascension strategy, which is something that you planned. Awakening is a process that is difficult, but once a Lightworker is awakened, there is no turning it off and you can set sail with a clear course.

Resources

www.sahvannaarienta.com

www.Newpagebooks.com

www.Soulsjourneyradio.com

www.Soulsjourneylightworkers.com

www.Soulsjourney.net

http://Templewithin.com

http://gatheringthunderfoundation.org

Index

About the Author

Sahvanna Arienta is an internationally known psychic medium, spiritual counselor, and author. Her unique style and connection to others is a powerful healing tool that has been a revolutionary force for change in the lives of her worldwide clientele. She is the author of *Lightworker: Understand your Sacred Role as Healer, Guide, and Being of Light* which has been called a transformational guide by many who have been overwhelmed with sensitivities and the empathic emotions that come with having unrecognized acute spiritual natures. Sahvanna resides in the northeast where she teaches workshops and seminars on healing and ascension strategies.